The Saints of S

Dominican Resistance in the Age of Neocolonialism

Ediciones Tito Montes
Movimiento Popular Dominicano

For information regarding this book contact Danny Shaw Columbia on Facebook or at DRS33@Columbia.edu

By Danny Shaw

Shedding that which is not Us
365 Days of Resistance: Standing on the Shoulders of Giants
The Saints of Santo Domingo
Diving over Infinite Horizons
My Son Blazes within Me

Dedication

This book is dedicated to Chu, Sagrario, Furi, Florinda, Maximiliano, Amín, Amaury, Manolo, Patria, Minerva, María, Onu, Victor, Dario, Bernardo, Braulio, Junior, Francisco, Rafael, Jacques, Cristian, Javier, Maritza, Moreno, Dagoberto, Enrique, Monica, Mayobanex, Otto, Hector, Fidel, Higinio, Richard, Emelia, Juan Carlos, Hipólito, Yolanda and all of the selfless warriors who gave everything in the struggle against tyranny. These young men and women embodied the élan of the MPD,[1] the new human material that Che wrote about. Unbreakable, steeled, integral, self-sacrificing and generous, they are and will always continue to be revolutionary optimists and the *voceros* or tribunes of the people! Because they could not be bought or corrupted, the enemies of freedom tried to silence them. These were our mentors whose examples and legacies live on in our resistance today. The *dirigentes* (leaders) of the future will be carved from the same steel. Without you, there could be no us. Your memory continues to haunt our exploiters. Our victory shall be yours before long *camaradas*!

---

[1] Organization formed by Dominican exiles in Cuba to overthrow the Trujillo dictatorship. This Marxist-Leninist organization continues to fight for a socialist Dominican Republic today and is one the subjects explored in this book.

Contents

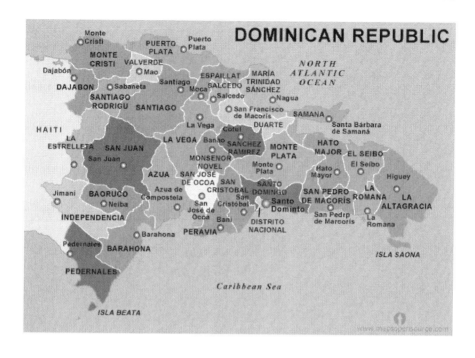

Introduction

Considering the dearth of critical writing in English on present day Dominican resistance, I felt an urgency to publish this book. I wrote the histories, poems, and articles that follow in the course of the last twenty years as I came of age —physically, intellectually and spiritually— in the Dominican Republic, Haiti and within the Dominican and Haitian diaspora in New York City. This book is an anti-imperialist Dominican reader, meant to counterpoise the deceptive, stereotypical misrepresentations that surround this Caribbean country of ten and a half million people.

From 1997 through the present day, I have been studying and learning Dominican Spanish and Haitian Kreyòl. In every *callejón* (alleyway), *loma* (mountain) and project hallway that I entered, I was armed with two perennial weapons —a pen and a pocket notepad. Every conversation and interaction contributed to my understanding of the social realities of the Dominican and Haitian people. At every stage of my intimacy with these two cultures, I wrote. Fifteen years after writing some of these reflections, I naturally saw my own words and thoughts differently. I edited my work but decided to let much of it stand as a testament to the anger and passions I felt as a young social observer, father, revolutionary and writer. The genre of writing shifts between narrative, social analysis, poetry and journalism, but the message of the book is consistent throughout; the need for profound change on both sides of the Caribbean Sea.

The Saints of Santo Domingo is organized into five sections.

In Section I. *Resistencia* (Resistance), I critically analyze the Dominican socio-economic and political landscape. I recount my experiences living, organizing and fighting alongside the Dominican revolutionary movement, spearheaded by the *Movimiento Popular Dominicano (MPD)*, a combat organization born of the stark social inequalities that characterize this Antillean society. The struggles highlighted in Section I., along with the almost mystical, larger-than-life protagonists the reader will discover, shaped me, my worldview and my relationship with the Dominican Republic. The opening section sets the stage for the chapters that follow and presents the most human portraits of the heroines and martyrs of the Dominican liberation struggle, for whom this book is named and to whom it is dedicated.

Section II. *Supervivencia* (Survival), and the following two sections, are comprised of poems that I wrote reflecting on the nefarious effects that imperialism —and its inevitable consequence, forced Dominican migration— have on the family, self-pride and identity building. Section II. highlights the everyday struggles of the Dominican people to forge a dignified existence in their besieged homeland.

Section III. *Éxodo* (Exodus) explores the dislocation of three generations of Dominicans from their nation. I capture the harrowing reality of involuntary migration. I then paint a social portrait of young exiles and their families adjusting to and surviving the streets of Washington Heights and the South Bronx. I included one poem that I wrote in Haitian Kreyòl because of the commonalities of the Dominican and Haitian migratory experience to New York City. Where I originally wrote a poem in Spanish or Haitian Kreyòl, I left the original text and then translated it into English.

Section IV. *Historia y Horizontes* (History & Horizons) revisits the legacy of the ancestors and revives the memory of figures whose work and example is relevant to present day struggles. Homage is paid to Dominican heroines and warriors who resisted (neo)colonial-backed tyranny. I have also included tributes to other fighters from outside of the Dominican Republic, whose life work mirrored the tasks of the unfinished Dominican revolution.

The final section, Section V. *Unidad* (Unity), is comprised of articles I previously published in newspapers and on websites in the Dominican Republic, Haiti and the U.S. Xenophobia, Haitian-Dominican relations, spiritual oppression and police brutality figure among the themes explored here. Three of these articles shift their attention to the Dominican Republic's closest neighbor and brother, Haiti. The first time I saw the Dominican military harass, interrogate, brutalize, separate and orphan Haitian families, I made a decision to learn Kreyòl. I knew that in order to stand in solidarity with the Haitian community and learn their story, I had to speak the venerable language of Boukman & Dessalines. The destiny of these two nations is intimately intertwined. Though today the two nations are separated by a militarized border, and on the Dominican side, from an internalized national chauvinism— future struggles promise to illuminate the necessity of Dominican-Haitian unity. In the words of Dominican poet Dió-genes Abreu, "without understanding *Haitianness,* we can never understand our *Dominicanness.*" My time on the border, travelling between the two countries and living in Haiti merits its own book. For now, I have interspersed my observations and experiences in Haiti in two of the chapters of The Saints of Santo Domingo.

Section I. Resistencia/Resistance

Stones and burning tires: the weapons of the poor

The Saints of Santo Domingo

Dominican Resistance in the Age of Neocolonialism

This past summer I returned to the Dominican Republic after a five year absence. I walked the streets of Navarrete, Santiago where I lived between 1997 and 2001. I was guided by a veteran MPD fighter, Amín, who walked with a limp because of a police bullet lodged into his right calf. We crisscrossed through the alley ways of La Mella, a working class district that was my old stomping grounds. We visited the homes of comrades who had matured with me, mentored me and adopted me into the underground movement fifteen years before. The nostalgia weighed heavy on me as I looked at the family portraits of fallen fighters. Before lunch, we had visited twelve homes. Four former leaders had been executed. One was paralyzed from the waist down. Two had become political prisoners. Three had been shot, incarcerated and tortured; they still militated in the movement. Two were in exile, one in Southern Florida, the other in Madrid. This was a microcosm of what the state had done to fractionalize and crush the MPD and El FALPO.

As I sat in an old fashioned rocking chair —in a modest living room, listening to the testimony of a proud mother and father, recounting the handsome, mischievous smile of their Socrates, a twenty year old warrior, slain by the military police— I vowed to tell their stories.

An Introduction

The memories that follow are not mine to tell. Nor is this the language in which these stories should be told, because it is not the language in which they were acted out on the historical stage. But the persecuted, the traumatized, the tortured, the incarcerated and the assassinated can no longer speak for themselves. The stories that follow are meant to eternalize their legacy.

The mere mention of the two revolutionary acronyms MPD and FALPO has the power to turn heads in the Dominican Republic. The MPD conjures up images of resistance from a bygone era when fearless heroes —emerging from the very bottom of society— confronted the dragoons of the ruthless dictators, Rafael Trujillo and Joaquín Balaguer. Hearing the five letters F-A-L-P-O, the Dominican psyche conjures up images of chaos, anarchy, work-stoppages, burning tires, confrontations with the police and looting. This is all too similar to what many Americans think of when they hear of Baltimore, Maryland or Ferguson, Missouri, the previously unheard of suburb of St. Louis, catapulted into the national spotlight after the police murder of unarmed eighteen-year-old Michael Brown and the consequent rebellion that raged on for months.

In the diaspora, the FALPistas are labeled as *tigueres* (gangsters or troublemakers) who initiate *huelgas* (strikes) and disorder to promote —as the narrative goes— their own narrow agenda.[2] In the pages that follow, I will share some of what I lived in the Dominican Republic alongside the MPD and El FALPO— two of the leading organizations mobilizing the poor and disenfranchised by demanding an overhaul of the economic order.

The Saints of Santo Domingo is meant to translate the MPD's worldview to the public in New York City and the U.S., a public that is at times very far away from Dominican reality but at other times, very close to it. These recollections give extension to the worldview, principles and examples of many remarkable fighters for the oppressed. These were young women and men who ignored risks, warnings and likely death. They didn't know how to live with caution because they were guided by conviction. With a saint-like devotion to their people, they sacrificed their own individual stability, and often their lives, to prosecute a just social transformation in their homeland.

---

[2] *Falpistas* are members of the FALPO, *Tigueres* is Dominican slang for thugs. *Huelgas* are strikes or shut-downs of the community.

Rojo y Negro: El MPD[3]

New York City is the epicenter of the one and half million strong Dominican diaspora in the United States. As an anti-imperialist organizer living in uptown Manhattan and the South Bronx, I came into contact with many exiled Dominican revolutionaries, a country I had barely heard of in my high school years. In 1997, I visited the Dominican Republic and Haiti for the first time and began working with the clandestine Movimiento Popular Dominicano (MPD) and its aboveground, popular front, El Frente Amplio de Lucha Popular (FALPO).[4] The FALPO was the open, democratic front of El MPD, organized in slums and towns across the country. Intermittently over the next twenty years, I lived and organized alongside the leadership of the Dominican movement, and at their side, sharpened my Afro-Caribbean Spanish and sociological understanding of Dominican society. I learned with them. I protested with them. I laughed with them. I mobilized with them. And I fought with them, forging deep bonds of lifelong friendship, solidarity and love.

My recollections will take the reader deeper into Dominican society, as I came to know it —far removed from the privatized white sand, beach resorts of Puerto Plata and Casa de Campo— and into the harsh economic and political context that gave birth to the fighters whose stories fill these pages. In New York City —home to some 800,000 Dominicans, the largest Dominican community outside of the D.R. —all too often Dominicans are reduced to a series of stereotypical character portraits. When the American public hears of the Dominican Republic, they think of beaches,

---

[3] Black and Red, the colors of the Cuban revolutionary movement, the Sandinista revolution and the MPD.

[4] Dominican Popular Movement and the Broad Front of Popular Struggle. Though I often use the two interchangeably, the MPD is the centrifugal force in the relationship. The FALPO –and every other popular front, such as the Peasant Front, the Women's Front or the Student Front (EL FELABEL) -receives its marching orders from the centralized apparatus, the MPD. Any youth, "down with the struggle," can be in the FALPO. Only the most serious leaders, who vowed to be unswerving professional revolutionaries, could join the MPD, that is the centralized Marxist-Leninist party.

tourism, rum and the Dominican fame for dancing and partying. Dominican Major League Baseball players have also become household names across the U.S. Did anyone ever stop to think: why did these players leave their homeland in the first place to play so far away? Why couldn't they be stars and idols in the land where they were born? The answer is a lot deeper than the cliché often repeated with imperial hubris, that "the U.S.A. has more opportunities and is the freest country in the world." The narratives that follow emerge from the underbelly of the thriving tourist enclaves to bear witness to a class-torn society in active revolt. Here you will discover true, real-life, Dominican heroes who have done much more than sing a song, win a dance contest or take a wooden stick and smack a ball hundreds of feet. In this book, you will meet the valiant, self-sacrificing young soldiers at the helm of an insurrection that threatens to topple Dominican class relations.

On the Organization of these Memoirs

The Saints of Santo Domingo weaves together disparate memories —some comical, others tragic, some heroic, others light-hearted. My account is based on true events. In order to protect the protagonists, I left out and changed many details. The reader will have to await a radical political rupture with the present ruling government of Danilo Medina and the poorly-named PLD (Dominican Liberation Party) before a complete history can be told. The names of the martyrs, when it does not bring harm to their families, remain the same, so that the reader can look deeper into what they stood for. The names of party wreckers, rapists, informants and murderers also remain the same, in hopes that the people's judgment will have the last word.

These memoirs are not necessarily chronological but rather appear as I remembered them, both within the diaspora and in the Dominican homeland.[5] I occasionally appear in the stories that

---

[5] Over the course of my work in the DR I fell in love and married a Dominican woman. We have a son together, Ernesto Rafael who is today 13 years old. I was

transpire. To the extent that I could, I removed myself from the unfolding events. My personal involvement in the unfolding Dominican liberation struggle provided depth to my perspective but did not skew it.

The Economic Forecast is Dismal with a Chance of Rocks

Navarrete —a city of 100,000 twenty minutes outside of Santiago by car— awoke to the sound of dozens of mothers and their children marching down the street banging on pots with aluminum spoons, demanding water and electricity. Three different generations of families demonstrated against the government-enforced austerity. Last night's revelers —carry the weight of rum-induced hang-overs— came into their doorways, squinting before the sun, observing eight-year-olds and thirteen-year-olds emulating the example of older rebels, militantly bouncing over the concrete and launching slogans against the status-quo.

What is the economic and social landscape that gives birth to so much rage and rebellion in the second largest country in the Caribbean? What would motivate mothers, grandmothers and cross sections of the community to come into the streets to protest?

The average salary of a Dominican worker pays a mere 53% of what economists calculate is the basic cost of living.[6] Over half of Dominican families, both in rural and urban settings, cannot survive on their salaries and are forced into the informal labor market to supplement their incomes. The national debt is an astonishing $34 billion dollars which is half of the Gross National Product.[7] The servile governments which have been in power since

---

adopted into her family and see them to this day as my own family. Here within, I refer to them as family members.

[6] "Wages of the Population do not Cover Basic Necessities." *El Dia* Newspaper. Senabris Silvestre. July 1st 2014.
[7] Statistic's taken from La Fuerza de la Revolucion's biannual report: published on August 17th 2014 and entitled "After Two Years of the PLD Government More of the Same with Minor Differences."

1966 loyally pay foreign banks to service a "national" debt which was contracted to enrich foreign corporations and their local lackeys. While Citibank, the International Monetary Fund and the World Bank ensure that the D.R. is hemorrhaging out billions of dollars in debt payments, the government systematically neglects necessary public services such as education, sanitation, public health and transportation. To this day, millions of Dominicans endure long stretches of the week waiting for running water and light. Unemployment —for the most economically-important members of society, between the ages of 18 and 40— hovers around the 50% mark. The basics of life are simply not viable for the vast majority in Dominican society. One day I asked one of my 12-year-old, *mulatta* nieces what she wants to be when she grows up? Her response: "A foreigner."

Working class families are presented with one of two options; migrate or hustle. Both immigration and crime statistics continue to climb in this nation of 10.5 million people. The Dominican Republic recorded the fourth largest remittances last year of all of the countries in Latin America and the Caribbean. The Dominican exile community in the United States sent $3.3 billion dollars back to their motherland.[8] If it were not for this gigantic assistance from Dominican workers in "the belly of the beast," the social pressure from below would be incalculably higher. How ironic. Assistance from the heart of the exploiter nation —the very metropolises which benefitted most from the centuries-long colonial theft of Dominican land, resources and labor power— is an escape valve which delays the inevitable combustion of such an inequitable society. What would happen if this financial lifeline were cut off?

At the same time that entire families and neighborhoods are forced to pack up and leave, the prison population continues to swell. Demoralized before the meager prospects of "making it," an increasing number of youth have turned to the drug trade and other extralegal activities. Fifteen years ago drugs were not as common and were rarely ever talked about, but today the nation of Duarte,

---

[8] "Dominican Republic is the 4th Largest Recipient of Remittances." *El Nacional*. June 10th 2014.

Sanchez and Mella (and so many other martyrs who remain out of the limelight for ideological reasons) is more dangerous than ever. The images of youth shot down by the police or rival drug dealers have become commonplace. Class contradictions push the society closer and closer to the precipice, threatening to plunge the masquerade of social peace and order into the abyss.

But where there is despair, there is rebellion. Repression breeds resistance. The devastating and disempowering poverty that is fertile breeding ground for both "criminals" and revolutionaries. The role of the MPD and its youth leadership in the FALPO is to steer the popular ire in the direction of protest and confrontation with the possessing class. The symbols of El FALPO are stones launched at the police and burning tires used as barricades to hold back the occupying army. From Gaza to Belfast, these are the time-honored weapons of the poor demanding to be recognized, respected and empowered with basic social and economic rights.

Camilo and Revolutionary Lesson Number #1

No matter how hot and humid it is, a professional Dominican revolutionary wears slacks, an ironed, button down shirt, and dress shoes. They are clean shaven, have a neat haircut and are professional in their demeanor and in their interactions with others. I arrived with the intention of wearing shorts and tank tops every day. This was not motivated so much by a "hippie" or anti-consumer style but was rather a 19-year-old's natural response to being overwhelmed by the sweltering heat of the Caribbean. It was not simply that it was 95 degrees but the fact that the humidity readings were consistently above 80%.

Every morning, for months, I boarded the *onza* (bus) in Villa Mella and got off forty five minutes later on Maximo Gomez Avenue —where I was hired to teach high-school history and economics— completely drenched in perspiration.[9] How could I

---

[9] Onzas were long public buses that were infamous for holding hundreds of passengers pressed together under the punishing sun with no AC to speak of.

work like this? But just as the American internationalist volunteers had to learn in Sandinista Nicaragua, I picked up very quickly that long hair, sandals, jean shorts and basketball gear would not cut it in the Dominican Republic. This was lesson #1. No one would take me seriously as a leader and I would be a permanent outsider, unless I presented myself professionally.

Camilo typified the conduct of a MPDista. He was extremely serious, kind, generous and humble. He was neat and meticulous in his dress. He read vociferously, devouring literature and world history. A human thesaurus, he introduced fresh words into everyone's vocabulary. Camilo had the highest honors in the Sociology Department at the *Universidad Autónoma, La U.A.S.D*, the oldest university of the Americas. When he came home after a twelve hour day, he visited ten to twenty families en route to his home. He checked how they were doing and delegated responsibilities to emerging leaders throughout the neighborhood. Armed with a stack of flyers, he coordinated the next face to face meeting and protest.

As he walked the narrow urban corridors of Villa Mella, he personified what it meant to be a sought-after revolutionary mentor, spokesperson and *dirigente popular*. The elderly loved him. Polite and attentive to their every need, Camilo was a soft-spoken, sweet young man. He adjusted his vocabulary, message and tone in order to win over every generation to meet the needs and demands of the national liberation struggle. With the youth he was a character and a comedian, rattling off witty and encouraging comments. He led study groups to sharpen the youth's sense of their national identity and their role in an international struggle. As a workhorse for freedom, Camilo set the tone of what it meant to be a MPDista and FALPista.

But when it was time to go in to battle to denounce impunity for corrupt politicians and murderous police agents, the *magna cum laude* transformed himself into an avenger of the poor. Tying a bandana over his face and trading polished black shoes for sneakers, he surged fourth into the streets, a one-man hurricane of people's war. When a comrade was shot in a protest, he ensured that three or more police shared a similar fate. Knowing no fear, he collected his fair share of scars from bullet wounds. At one point he was in a wheel chair for over a year. He never complained or felt self-pity. His smile and socialist zeal never faded; he only grew more emboldened.

After Camilo's house was ambushed and he narrowly escaped the would-be assassin's bullets, the party moved him out of his neighborhood deeper into the countryside. The MPD's highest leadership body —the Central Committee (CC)— knew that President Leonel Fernandez's government had placed a red x on Camilo's back. He was a marked man. Still, he led every demonstration. He tracked down every sell-out. He escaped from every prison. He went into hiding but always emerged again to lead the next struggle. To his peers and detractors alike, he was indomitable.

But one day mortality caught up with him. The entire neighborhood knew the military was coming for him. He was ordered to remain in a safe house far away from La Capital. Even in hiding, his intensity and commitment remained ablaze. This would prove to be his downfall. He secretly travelled back to Los Guaricanos in Villa Mella and was spotted. A snitch tipped off the police to where the safe house was. The raid that followed was swift and heavy. Every last layer of the state —uniformed and undercover— equipped with heavy and small arms, surrounded the safe house. He was blown to smithereens before he could even get a single shot off. For good measure, the military police murdered another leader's two cousins who were apolitical but just happened to be in the targeted home. Fortunately, the rest of the family was not near the safe house at the time or they too would have taken their place among the martyred, so that the state could bolster its message.

To this day, those that knew him are overwhelmed by love and nostalgia when they remember the lessons they learned by Camilo's side. He was too talented, fearless, free and pure for this world. He had an angelic-like quality to him. If only future generations could have borne witness to his character and complete sense of dedication. To know him was to be touched. He surrendered all of his talents so that up-and-coming generations could tap into their talents and the squelched potential of a blockaded nation.

Though their coffins may settle, their spirits only ascend.[10]

The Most Furious

Furi was the most fearless and *furioso* of all, hence his nickname. The government outlawed the MPD's black and red flag from the outset of the founding of the "illegal" party in 1959, in the years of the Trujillo dictatorship. 3,000 leftist leaders were executed in the twelve years of terror at the order of the dictator Joaquín Balaguer. *La Banda Colorá* was formed as an anti-communist death squad to hunt down and destroy the leftist leaders.[11] The military burnt the MPD's national office to the ground in 1981. While there is no official tally, the state murdered hundreds of youth, student,

---

[10] Translation of Manuel Del Cabral's poem.
[11] The Red Gang, in reference to the color of Joaquín Balaguer's Reformist Party.

union and popular leaders over the decades, for daring to defy the previously described neoliberal inequality.

To fly the black and red flag was to be a sworn enemy of the state. And this is exactly what Furi was. At any given demonstration or even at the *fiestas patronales* (regional fair), he unfurled the flag in plain view of all, inviting the police or anyone to confront him.[12] It must be reemphasized that as of 2005, the MPD and its symbol —the red and black flag— were illegal. His comrades reasoned with him to bring the flag home before there was a shootout.

With a humbug's grin and a used car salesman's insistence, Fury refused. Fiery and young, he was ready to trade lead with the police at any moment. A member of the CC and a veteran of the guerrilla war in Colombia cautioned him: "We are not just dangerous because of that heat" —motioning towards his belt— "but because of this heat," pressing two of his fingers to Furi's head. He posed a pivotal question: "What separates us from those common delinquents?" as he pointed to a crew of *Dominicanyorks* with beer bottles in their hands.[13] He placed his index finger on Furi's head and then pointed to his heart: "Our vision of the future and our love for the underdog."

The police took one look at Furi with his broad shoulders, stocky build and confidence and vacillated before entering into any confrontation with him. On one occasion, MPD counter-intelligence, which had infiltrated the state, gave him a heads up that the military was coming for him. "The Most Furious" stayed up two nights straight, on his porch, clutching an automatic weapon. He sent a message: they can take me but I'm taking a dozen of them with me. Veteran leaders reasoned with him again: "Furi: your life is worth more than a dozen or even a thousand of these goons and sycophants. Go into hiding. Let things simmer down." But Furi's

---

[12] Regional celebrations with live music, food and the carnival like atmosphere to celebrate the patron saints of each province.

[13] *Dominicanyorks* is a Spanglish term for Dominicans residing in New York with access to US dollars who return home on vacation and have a mentality that they are better than the locals because their money is now worth more.

head was harder than a coconut. He had signed his own death sentence. Everyone lived in denial that Furi could ever be taken away because he appeared invincible.

Youth: Sacrificed

One Saturday after an anti-drug workshop in *la 27 de Febrero* neighborhood, a group of *compañeros* stayed up all night sharing beers, *malanga, yucca and platanos*, three types of *viveres* or roots common in the Dominican diet.[14] This was the first night that Furi and his girlfriend from the student movement were alone together. They were locked away a few rooms from us making love for the first time. In between one song which ended and before another began, we heard intermittent sonorous notes of passion emerge from the room.

Furi's girlfriend, Diana was shockingly beautiful; collecting glances and compliments everywhere she went.Diana had invented an alibi, telling her family that she was going away for a university fieldtrip in the mountains. The next morning —draped in the most wry, school-boy of grins— Furi embellished about his all night exploits. He was proud to say he had fired off eight shots, referring to how many times he had ejaculated. The comrades joked that "they better get on their horses to keep up with Furi and his superhuman communist exploits." These all too human moments made the soldiers temporarily forget that there was a war being unleashed upon their ideals and convictions. In these touching moments of "normality," university-aged students deceived themselves to believe they had their entire lives ahead of them.

The reality check was not far off. It was 4 a.m. when the invasion came. Furi was fast asleep. He was blown away in his bed and executed the way Fred Hampton was thirty two years before.[15] The military police came at the most cowardly hour because they

---

[14] Compañero or its abbreviation compa means comrade.
[15] Reference to the FBI and Chicago Police Department's execution of Black Panther Party Chairman Fred Hampton in 1969.

knew they stood no chance if Furi was awake. It was the dawn of January 5th, 2002. Thirty bullets later, another leader was barely recognizable. Furi was 22 years old.

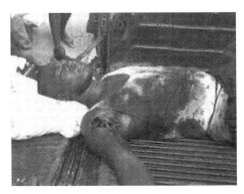

Months later, his girlfriend, Diana participated in a march for student rights. The Dominican left's international anthem roared off of a sound truck. *"Casas de Carton"* (Cardboard homes) was Los Guaraguao's song that stood as a stirring portrait of poverty in Venezuela and all of Latin America.[16] As she marched behind the sound truck, her hands clapping to the beat of the triumphant song, her stomach appeared bigger. She was pregnant with a young Furi. The world was pregnant with resistance.

Barahona's *Bachatu*[17]

Dominican life is a transnational journey that zig-zags back and forth from the streets of Santo Domingo to the South Bronx and from Salcedo to South Florida. Almost every Dominican family has relatives in Uptown Manhattan, the Bronx, Lawrence, Massachusetts, Southern Florida and the Eastern Seaboard, who send money home to support loved ones. Migration is a survival strategy that divides millions of families. It is no wonder Dominican families give a round of applause to the pilot every time they arrive back

---

[16] https://www.youtube.com/watch?v=f1m6jgWUYko
[17] Barahona is a town in the dry desert like South of the Dominican Republic. Bachatu is a dancer or singer of the national bachata music.

home on a flight from the United States. In some cases, ten or twenty years have elapsed since they saw their parents or children.

Many organizers were forced to migrate because of financial necessity, others because of political repression. Joaquín Flores's story was born of this reality.

Joaquín was my revolutionary passport to Barahona. He was my English student on 134th street in Washington Heights at the Roberto Clemente center. We taught each other slang phrases in our respective languages. I still have a torn, half sheet of paper with his writing:

1. *Esta fiesta fue de pinga.*[18]
2. *Dime bacano, que lo que?*
3. *Nitido!*
4. *Dame luz manín!*

After a few classes, he could tell from my teaching and conversational style that I came out of what we call "the movement." He told me his story and we grow closer as friends.

His main focus was on being a player and scooping up girls with his renowned *bachata* dance moves. They do not make them any smoother than Joaquín. He invited me to accompany him to Bronx house parties and dance clubs that were packed until the sun came up. I could not keep up with his drinking and dancing but in my quest to build up my knowledge of the Dominican dialect, I stayed into the early hours of the morning, absorbing the ambiance and social interactions.

Joaquín lived in a massive, pentagon-shaped public housing complex on 135th street and Broadway. There were over 700 families in that New York City tenement, the population of many towns upstate. We took the elevator up to the 27th floor where he

---

[18] Slang terms meaning
1. That party was the shit.
2. What's good my n*&^%?
3. Word! Or Fresh!
4. Tell me what's going down young blood!

lived with his aunt, uncle and cousins. He motioned to two young women walking through the lobby. He bragged that he gave them $100 to go to their apartments to sleep with them. In one breath, he explained the *prietas* were the best in bed and in the next how he would link me up with revolutionaries in his hometown, when I travelled to D.R.[19] He grew up surrounded by revolutionaries in *el Barrio Mamá Tingó* and had never lost touch with them. The police shot him in his behind, ironically during a demonstration against police brutality. Thanks to family in Manhattan, he fled the country to have surgery in the U.S. because he feared the police would target him and track him down in the public hospital. In 1999, he fled Barahona for New York City.

Arriving at the end of my teenage years, Joaquín was my introduction to Dominican nightlife. One night Joaquín gulped down too much *mamajuana* (moonshine). The most peaceful rascal on earth was instantly transformed into a perverted devil. He was insulting and obnoxious. He was falling over the women at a family gathering. The elders in the room signaled for us to get him out of there to a safe place. They saw us to the door and I scooped him up over my shoulder and we made an inglorious exit. It was one thing to get him down the stairs but once we were on 137th street my arms and shoulders gave out. Unintentionally, I dropped him into a snow bank. I didn't know what to do. I couldn't carry him anymore. The snow was at least softer than the concrete entrance of McDonalds. Joaquín started to motion like a snow angel muttering some drunken, nostalgic nonsense about Christopher Columbus, the Arawaks and flying back to save them from genocide. Even in his drunken stupor, he was speaking to me about the need for a stronger movement. Then, our beloved snow angel began to vomit on himself. I flipped him over but he was only semi-conscious. I called the paramedics. They brought him to a hospital bed at Columbia Presbyterian hospital. When he was receiving his IV, completely unconscious, other friends came and met me to see him in the hospital. Observing his inebriated state, they invited me to another party. We spent the night in revelry then went back to sleep in the chairs alongside his

---

[19] *Prietas* means Black women (in this case African American women) and can be offensive or not depending on the tone and context of the speaker's voice.

hospital bed. He woke up the next morning —as jolly as could be—with all of us at his side. He swore we were "the most loyal friends" on earth.

Joaquín embodied the contradictions within a liberation movement vying for a different future but emerging from a backward past. One of Washington Heights premier "players" had a police bullet lodged into his rear end. He was part of a "huelga" and was preparing to launch a Molotov cocktail when he was shot. He was not a socialist per se but he grew up in a milieu where participating in street protests and disturbances was the thing to do. He was known for anti-gay and anti-women jokes which were in direct conflict with his socialist training.

In New York City, Joaquín settled into the routine of an everyday exploited factory worker in Hunts Point, without any interest of the wider class struggle. Battered down by his own reality, he had no energy left to wage a struggle to liberate others. His drinking became more frequent and he aged at twice the speed he had aged when he was in his native land. Joaquín would never completely adapt to this strange foreign land but without a visa to exit and come back, he, like so many of his contemporaries, was stuck.

When he learned that I was traveling to his hometown, he instructed me to go see Barahona's popular commander, Quibio Estrella.[20] Little did I know, I would be entering into contact with revolutionaries with whom I would be establishing life-long friendships and an unbreakable camaraderie. The survivors of exploitation, evictions and exile were my revolutionary passport to fly back and meet the chief protagonists in the unfolding drama of the Dominican Republic's national liberation struggle.

---

[20] Barahona is a city of 140,000 in the south of the D.R.

"Dime Líder!"[21]

When I arrived in Quibio's territory, he kept his distance from me, sizing me up. The bus dropped me off at a rest stop. Two young men arrived on a *pasola* (moped) across the highway. Quibio was on one of them staring at me through the speeding cars and motorcycles with another *compañero* named Sandi. I am not sure who he was expecting but I could see he was second-guessing the idea of picking up this 6'6" clean shaven, light-skinned stranger from the United States. I motioned for him to cross the highway with his entourage. He approached with a cautious smile; "Who sent you to Barahona? The CIA?" *Good one* I think. *I've only heard that sarcastic remark 100 times.* Accustomed to the half-teasing jokes, I matched his quick wit with my own. "Yes. They told me to come find Quibio Estrella, the most dangerous man in all of Barahona. They promised to compensate me fairly if I brought Balaguer your head." He cracked up and the initial tension was eased. He sped off with the three of us on his moped. I was sitting in the middle. Another *pasola* soon trailed closely behind. I was afraid my height and weight would upset the balance and we would wipe out, but I quickly learned about Dominicans' adroit skills balancing overcrowded mopeds.

Quibio and his lieutenants addressed one another using *compañero* or *líder*. It was a revolutionary form of greeting that differentiated them from everyone else. Our next stop was a stationary store. Quibio burst in: "Fellow Freedom Fighters! The revolutionaries of the future have arrived. We need your attention. We need 500 flyers, tape, glue, and whatever else you can spare and collaborate with. We will give you $1/4^{th}$ up front. Another $1/4^{th}$ when things settle after the strike. Can you donate the rest?" Was it intimidation at work or genuine solidarity? The store clerks consented, flew into action and after some light cajoling we were off to our next assignment. Quibio ran this town like an insurgent Jesse James on the Western frontier.

That night four *compañeros* glued signs and spray painted the party's message everywhere. Two FALPistas stood guard while

---

[21] "What's up Leader!"

someone else held the posters and the other painted glue across it. The red and black graffiti declared "*National Strike Friday*," "*Only the People can Save the People*" and "*Yankees out of the Dominican Republic*." Sandi, who was keeping watch, took hits from a pocket size bottle of rum. Why they let him drink "on the job?" Another *vocero* (spokesperson) explained, "Yeah, we have a few of those. Loyal as hell to the cause, but big drinkers. We do our best to weigh on him but he is a *cabeza dura*."[22]

The alcohol issue came up often. A few days later, I was invited to give a talk to fifty youth at a retreat at a river in the mountains. They had brought two boxes of *Barcelo* rum for the *pasadia*.[23] I questioned the leadership's decision: "This is how we are going to organize the future fighters to take on Leonel's government?" We entered into a polemic about Dominican youth and their idiosyncrasies. I was clearly outnumbered. They said if it weren't for the alcohol and the laid back atmosphere, 80% of them would not have come.

Now it was my turn to talk. I was introduced as a sociologist and revolutionary leader from the heart of the empire. Ever-conscious of my surroundings and crowd, I realized that I was all that stood between the group of youth and their *moro*, rum and freedom.[24] I stepped up like a fighter into the ring and articulated a quick ten minutes of historical and ideological daggers at imperialism and its ability to pit oppressed people against one another as the rich get away scot-free with that which belongs to us. After hearing me speak, they wanted to know if we combat the police with gunfire and shut down New York City like they do. "Not with as much militancy at this historical juncture but we *get it in* too," I assured them.[25] Later the *compas* joked with me: "That was no workshop. That was no cultural exchange. That was a call to insurrection."

---

[22] *Voceros* are the elected spokespeople and *cabeza dura* is a hard head.
[23] Fieldtrip.
[24] Rice with the beans and seasoning cooked in.
[25] We get it in is slang for carrying something out with fervor.

The hours passed by. Everyone hung out. I met a pretty and articulate law student from la U.A.S.D. We shared, smiled and connected. She offered me a cup of rum. To me it was an insult. I was still so young and naive. I had yet to transcend the phase of thinking revolutionaries were machines without these human impulses, temptations and vices. I tossed the rum she had offered me into the trees behind me and walked away. I was rude to her. I was nineteen at the time. It would take me years to comprehend how even the saints have their all-too-human habits. Transcending this dogmatic ultra-leftist phase would be part of my growth.

Transcending the Trauma

Everyone was in a festive mood and took a dip in the river. The entire left side of Quibio's body was bandaged. Massive scar tissue lined that side of his body. Later on in the night, Quibio told his story to comrades who were visiting from out of town:

> *"Coño Líder como te digo?*[26] *It was two summers ago. We prepared for a strike that would shut down the entire province. By strike of course I mean the complete shutting down of the province's economy, traffic...everything. Foreign companies from Canada and the US rob our nickel and gold deposits, leaving us only with the toxic waste remnants. We tried to shut down their mining operations but the police had blocked the main streets to the mine entrance. We went to battle and we took a half dozen of those sorry police bastards out. They grabbed me on one of the main boulevards. After beating me to a pulp they took an unburnt tire and threw it on top of me like a necklace. It was laced with gasoline and they lit it on fire. It burnt half of my body. This happened to three of us who were at the head of the strikes in those years. Pengüino went to Cuba to get treatment. Thomás escaped to the Bronx. The compañeros*

---

[26] "Fuck How can I break this down to you leader?"

chipped in and I was able to get some treatment here. None of us were ever the same after. We are still cadre. We never missed a beat in the streets but socially...well you can imagine trying to be with a woman."

His story spoke of the enormous sacrifices the leaders endured. The lives of these three strapping, young lads were changed forever, and yet backing down was still never an option.

A Tribune of the People

Arriving from a different world, it appeared that our protagonists suffered from paranoia. They took every precaution, never travelling the same route and never sleeping in the same bed. I learned through concrete experience that this was their cold reality. When the movement convoked meetings, it was better to do them in completely public places or completely underground locations. Something in between gave the state ample room to infiltrate the meetings and potentially ambush them. After witnessing the police trails and informants, who constantly badgered the *dirigentes populares*, the security protocol made complete sense.

The night after the retreat, we gathered for a meeting. It was late and Quibio and his entourage prepared to leave the associate's house where I was staying. The *vocero* always had two or three impromptu body guards with him for security purposes. The police were waiting downstairs. As the leaders exited, one of Quibio's closest mentees reached for his pistol, thinking he would shoot it out before going off to jail peacefully. Quibio calmly pushed the bodyguard's hand back down away from the firearm, giving him a look as if to say *Why would we squander vital resources and lives on these robots and puppets when we have an entire war of liberation to prosecute.* The entourage was rounded up without an explanation and arrested. I had been Quibio's guest in Barahona for 72 hours and had yet to experience a dull moment. How eye-opening to be a part of it all.

The next day the movement was called to action and there was a protest in front of the police headquarters demanding their release. When Quibio strode triumphantly out of police headquarters, hundreds of youth and community members cheered his liberation. He mounted a police car and spoke to the sprawling multitude. Confident and untouchable, his twenty years of experience as an agitator was recognizable. You could hear a pin drop as his words bellowed out into humid air, charging the police with being the hired thugs of the Falconbridge LTD. Gold mining company. He was their leader, the pride of Barahona, and no one was going to steal him from them.

The Masters of the Dominican Economy

What plagues the D.R. is not scarcity but greed and opulence, in a word capitalism. The Dominican people collectively produce over $101 billion dollars in goods and services every year.[27] From the point of view of economists —who measure the growth of the Gross Domestic Product— the economy is booming. There is more than enough production to satisfy the needs and dreams of the 10.5 million Dominicans in the country and those economically-induced into exile abroad, including a million and a half who live in the U.S., over fifty thousand in Spain and tens of thousands of others who live in Puerto Rico, Venezuela, Canada and beyond.

[27] CIA World Factbook country report. 2013.

So where does all this money go? Why is there vast poverty for enormous sections of the population? Who is to blame for the mis-organization of the economy?

The answer lies with an elite group of massive corporations and billionaires that lay claim to the lion's share of the nation's wealth. Economist and author Cesar Augosto Sencion Villalona wrote a document in which he analyzed the class forces at play in Dominican society.[28] He reported that in the entire country there were a mere 145,653 bosses or supervisors, less than 5% of the population. The other 95% of the population was comprised of wage workers, informal workers, farmers, housewives, small property owners and the petty bourgeoisie. A history of uninterrupted foreign exploitation left the most vulnerable sections of the toiling class no option but to sell their labor power to the vampire-like foreign and domestic capital. In its economic development report of the country Forbes bragged:

> *"The D.R. has been declared the top-ranking cigar exporter to the U.S., the number one exporter of organic cocoa and organic bananas to Europe, and the world's fifth-largest supplier of beer and sugarcane rum. It is also the tenth-largest footwear exporter and the 22nd-largest exporter of apparel and textiles to the U.S. That's not a bad record for a Caribbean island with a population of nearly ten million."*

This is indeed a good record from the perspective of one class and an embarrassment and anti-national record from the view of the other class. Millions of Dominican workers pour their life blood into the main industries that make the Dominican Republic profitable for investors; sugar processing, ferronickel, gold mining, textiles, cement and tobacco. The average salary for a Dominican worker in these industries is roughly $850 dollars a year. The world's leading gold-mining company, the Barrick Gold Corporation, has billions of dollars invested in extracting gold,

---

[28] Program of La Fuerza de la Revolucion. February 2011.

nickel and other valuable metals. The workers, who risk life and limb for their profits, earn a mere pittance of what these precious metals fetch on international markets. Franklin Sports, Fruit of the Loom and Adidas owned Dick's Sporting Goods are among the largest exploiters of sweatshop labor in the country, paying as low as an abysmal $32/week or about $0.73/hour. Some 378,000 Dominicans work in these sweatshops. Today's neocolonial profits come on the heels of yesterday's colonial enslavement. Failure to understand this history obfuscates the present moment.

In the neo-colony, foreign capital works hand and hand with the national bourgeoisie. Here follows a list of the richest families in D.R. This illustrious group is composed of virtually all white or light-skinned older males who trace their roots back to Spain, Italy and other colonizing nations. For most of the billionaires —under the column source of wealth— it reads inheritance. In other words, the lords of the Dominican destiny, trace their billions back to the colonial economy, the plantation and enslaved Black labor.

The Bourgeoisie and their businesses in the D.R.

No	Family Name	# of Big Businesses
1	Vicini-Cabral	40
2	Bonetti	24
3	Barceló	13
4	Viyella San Miguel	22
5	Corripio Estrada	45
6	Cáceres-Troncoso	17
7	Brugal	30

8	León Asensio	23
9	Armenteros	37
10	Haché	20
11	Vitienes	31
12	Pellerano-Ricardt	50
13	Báez-Romano	19
14	Bermúdez	54
15	Najri	21
16	Lama	20
	Total	**467**

Source: Rosario, Esteban: The Masters of the Dominican Republic. Los dueños de la República Dominicana. June 2008.

Casa de Campo

The case of the Fanjul brothers —Cuban Americans based out of Southern Florida, considered by Forbes one the richest families in the US— shows for whom the economic landscape in the DR is favorable. The Fanjuls own not only sugar cane plantations in Central Romana but also the highly-acclaimed tourist resort Casa de Campo. Casa de Campo is its own world occupying five miles of coveted real estate in the southeast coast of the Dominican Republic. Casa de Campo has fourteen swimming pools, dozens of the most modern golf courses, $1,000 a night villas and its own private security force. Unless a local is a waitress, maid, security guard or entertainer, a native would not even think of trying to penetrate the gated fortress reserved for the Dominican elite and rich, mostly white tourists. The Fanjuls also own hundreds of thousands of acres of sugar plantations in Southern Florida where their workers produce Domino sugar. They have had close associations with right wing politicians and white supremacy groups.[29] They are emblematic of the other sixteen families listed in the chart above.

Such opulence defies reason. There is a mind-blowing gap between what workers receive and what the owners of these companies claim as profits. It is this wealth, created from the nation's resources and an exploited people's labor power that is in dispute. No matter how many public relations firms and lawyers the Vicinis and Fanjuls hire, there is no way to reconcile their interests with those of the producing class.

President Danilo Medina and the government's silence are to be expected. Like all of the presidencies before them, they function as little more than the political representatives and defenders of big money. When Juan Bosch's government attempted to lightly challenge this paradigm winning the first democratic election in the nation's history in 1963, imperialism quickly flexed its muscles. The story of why the nation does not progress is more complicated than political corruption which is indubitably rampant. But these are crumbs compared to what is stolen in an open, legal way. The politicians in power are backed up by the might of the ruling class and actively persecute grass-roots organizations. The Dominican Republic then is not a democracy but a dictatorship of the rich. The servile class also services an $18 billion debt to imperialist banks such as the International Monetary Fund and World Bank. After centuries of strangling the economic potential of the oppressed, dependent country, high finance insists on collecting an astronomical amount of the GDP to "service the debt." Contrary to the propaganda, the flow of resources and money is not from the North to the South but rather the opposite.

The contradiction between the creation and ownership of wealth is the central one plaguing D.R. and every oppressed country.

---

[29] "Billionaires won't fire assistant for KKK link." *New York Post*. October 9th 2010.

The MPD seeks to overthrow this robber-baron class and the state that protects them. Anything short of this, they consider a denial of justice for the Dominican people.

Globalization or Humiliation?

I went to a beach with my partner, Yuberkys in Puerto Plata, not far from Navarrete, when we were first dating. We exited the water and I limped to our towel due to a hair line fracture that I received fighting in New York State Golden Glove championships. A military guard stood guard, looking for "riffraff" (read working class, dark-skinned locals), remarked "Diablo trigueña cogiste ese gringo tan duro que esta cojo."[30] Looked over at me, disgusted, Yuberkys was accustomed to the disrespect. She commented: "Did you hear him? He thinks I'm your prostitute. What are you going to do?" His assumption was that I did not speak a word of Spanish and that I was using Yuberkys for momentary pleasure.

The signs outside of the beach read "Private property. No trespassing." This can be understood as meaning reserved for foreigners. The finest most pristine beaches of the world were reserved for foreigners. How much had things changed from the epoch of the plantation economy?

---

[30] "Damn mulata colored girl you fucked that gringo so hard he is limp."

International finance through the IMF and World Bank has rendered Dominican currency almost worthless before the euro or dollar. Any run of the mill worker in the US suddenly becomes a man of great value in the exploited nations. This is why the *El Malecón, El Conde* and other tourist destinations have a spate of old European and American men who come to purchase short term girlfriends on a weekly or monthly basis. The tourists' right to prey upon Dominican flesh was protected with police batons and battalions. Any interference with the serenity and superiority of the tourist landed a Dominican behind bars. A German tourist walked calmly down a main boulevard in Puerto Plata with nothing on below his waist. His shirt descended loosely covering his bratwurst-belly but his private parts were in plain view for everyone to see. Where is the respect for women's rights? Where is the dignity of the nation? Where is the sovereignty? Where is the independence?

In contrast to the exultation of the white tourist and neo-colonizer, Haitians are the most common target of Dominican frustrations. Samson was a guest at our wedding. My running mate for years, he was one of my first Kreyòl teachers. Some uncles of my bride to be took it upon themselves to escort him out of the wedding and throw him in the street. They were wanna-be bouncers and *guatchiman!*[31] They claimed they thought the "smelly Haitian had wandered in, uninvited, off the streets." Silent before the true invaders, the colonized misdirect their anger towards those who are even worse off. The over one million Haitians, forced to eke out a living over the border live in apartheid like conditions. I dedicated myself to learning Kreyòl to break down the barriers that have been artificially erected between two nations who share a common enemy.[32] The final chapter of this book will deal more directly with Haiti's own quest for self-determination.

---

[31] Dominican Spanglish term that comes from their pronunciation of night watchman.

[32] To read my work on this subject see these two articles from *Haiti Liberte* newspaper: "Passages to Haiti" and "El Anti-Haitianismo: An Ideology of Racial Inferiority" which I authored under the name Daniel or Danyel Peña-Shaw.

Backyardism[33]

The Dominican Republic, like other Caribbean and Latin American nations who have yet to cut the umbilical cord that connects them to their old masters, is a neo-colony; an extension of US transnational's business objectives. In 1823, the Monroe Doctrine declared Latin American and the Caribbean the US's backyard and signaled for Spain and other old colonial powers to recognize that there was a new empire to be reckoned with. Last year US secretary of state, John Kerry declared that the Monroe Doctrine was over. How noble! After nearly 200 years of foreign domination, a leading imperialist spokesperson had the audacity to say the US no longer sought to openly control and pillage the region. His statement was more of a reflection of Latin America's standing up to the empire —led by Venezuela, Bolivia, Ecuador and others— than the U.S.'s voluntary surrender of control.

Today the DR stands on the opposite pole of Venezuela and the leftist trend in Latin America. To describe the Dominican Republic as an independent nation is to strip the word independence of any real significance. The Dominican Republic has little more than what Frantz Fanon called "flag independence." The true decisions about the economic and political organization of the life of the nation are made in far off boardrooms in Washington D.C. and Wall Street. Whenever the D.R. threatened to challenge foreign control, U.S. marines invaded to put the right people back in power.

From 1916 to 1924 U.S. marines occupied DR and trained the ruthless and notorious General Rafael Trujillo to carry out their will for the next three decades. They used Trujillo to do their bidding and carried out a gruesome repression of any forces who dared to stand up to them. *Los gavilleros* were peasants who were pushed off of their land by US sugar monopolies and organized themselves as guerrillas against the foreign usurpers. After Trujillo's death, there was again a democratic groundswell from below. Democratic elections were organized for the first time in the history of the country and Professor Juan Bosch, a liberal, left

---

[33] Reference to US policy makers belief that the Caribbean constituted the US empire's backyard.

candidate was elected president. Bosch sought to enact land reform and pass a minimum wage law. On April 28th, 1965 42,000 US marines invaded to restore the dictatorship of the rich. The Lyndon Baines Johnson administration expected the occupation of the Caribbean nation of 3.9 million to be a cakewalk. A dogged popular resistance —led by disaffected army coronels Francisco Caamaño and Rafael Fernandez Dominguez— pinned down the post-WW II U.S. hegemon in "another Vietnam," to use Ernesto Guevara's tri-continental rallying cry. In the famous "War of April," Dominican patriots united together in defense of the constitution and their president, waging a popular war against the invasion. The U.S. tilted the balance of forces, slaughtering an untold amount of Dominicans who opposed their military intervention in internal Dominican affairs. To this day, the Dominican dead have yet to be counted and the U.S. government has never officially recognized or apologized for the heinous crimes they committed.

In the War of April, never was the divide clearer between the interests of empire and the interests of the people. Post-occupation, the U.S. handpicked and endorsed the puppet president, Joaquín Balaguer. Balaguer oversaw the notorious "12 years of terror" from 1966-1978 liquidating journalists, unionists, and leftists alike who criticized the latest stage of Trujillismo. This was all done with the US's support in the name of democracy. Much has been written about the two U.S. occupations of D.R. in the 20th century and the bloodthirsty dictators that the occupiers shepherded into power, Rafael Trujillo and his intellectual right hand man, Joaquín Balaguer. Although Trujillo was assassinated in 1961 by U.S. intelligence services, after he was officially deemed untrustworthy, and Balaguer passed away from old age in 2002, the legacy of Trujillismo and Balaguerismo remained. Little has been written — and still less translated into English— about the state repression that persisted against the Dominican left in the years of formal democracy. This book stands as a witness to the repression of a generation that insisted on challenging impunity. Like young Black men hunted by the police in the cities of the US, the average life expectancy of the FALPistas was young, far too young.

"El Moreno"

May 23rd 2001 was the 29th anniversary of the assassination of the legendary Marxist Dominican leader, Maximiliano Gomez "El Moreno" (the Black man). El Moreno was the Carlos Fonseca or Ho Chi Minh of the national liberation struggle in Santo Domingo. A humble giant, he was the Secretary General of the MPD. His life and exploits merited an entire biography unto itself. He was almost never mentioned in the Dominican media or school system because the powerful feared his legacy.

El Moreno came of age in the *bateys* or sugar cane fields of San Pedro de Macoris, the same town that has given birth to so many famous baseball players. He borrowed his sister's shoes to go to school because his family could not afford another pair. He organized the cane workers against their bosses, emerging as a union leader. He was ultimately elected the national Secretary General of the underground workers party, the MPD. Copies of revolutionary books were smuggled back and fourth among El Moreno and the MPD cadre so that they could sharpen their political analysis. Kryptonite to the nation's oppressors, these ideas were outlawed. The underground party workers ripped the cover off of the banned books to make it harder for the National Guard to know what they were reading, if they were caught. Books had to be buried in secret backyard locations. Activists were killed just because they were caught with literature that bore the names Marx, Lenin, Mao, Galeano, or Harnecker.

Maximiliano Gomez emerged as the leading synthesizer of his generation of the unfolding class struggle. He combatted the US invasion of the Dominican Republic in 1965 before becoming a political prisoner. In a daring maneuver to set their prisoners free, other MPDistas kidnapped a CIA agent and American Coronel, Donald Crowley in 1970. In a prisoner exchange, he was released in exchange for 20 MPD prisoners, including El Moreno. El Moreno was immediately forced into exile. Shortly after the audacious abduction, the Secretary General of the MPD was murdered by Dominican and US intelligence agents who used gases to poison him during the first days of his exile in Brussels. None of Balaguer's henchmen were ever prosecuted for their murderous crimes.

Reinventing Space

El Moreno was a towering figure, a model life to admire and emulate. The annual tributes to El Moreno's life brought hundreds of MPD'istas to the capital from around the country to celebrate his legacy.

A cadre who was a teacher in the capital was called upon to host twenty young FALPistas from Licey and Navarrete. How all these teenage revolutionaries in training would fit in a one room flat was unclear. The *compañeros* hosted one another around the country, never hesitating to share whatever they had with their FALPO family. By 2 a.m., things became clearer. No one was going to sleep. The crew of *campesino* (peasant) leaders wandered the *malecon* (coastal waterfront) the entire night. Many of the youth from the two different provinces had never left their hometowns before. They explored, laughed and shared the little money they could pool together. The high school teacher's salary of a few hundred dollars a month could only go but so far for so many people but it afforded the visitors an excellent night out in the capital.

Fifteen years later, the party analyzed who migrated? Who sold out to the government? Who was kidnapped, tortured or gunned down? How many of those young men are still revolutionaries who emulate "El Moreno?" It was impossible to keep track of everybody but herein, some of their stories are recuperated.

"Un Lumpen"

The lumpen proletariat is a Marxist term for the most marginalized sectors of society. Unable to find work, the "cast off" resort to prostitution, drug-dealing or any form of "extra-legal" hustling. In the Dominican left, the term means just this but also refers to everyday thugs and dope dealers.

The revolution —as it gathers momentum— attracts the best and worst of society. Everyone wants to be part of the winning team. There are those who seek to make their careers off of the chaos. Everyone wants to jump on the bandwagon to get a piece of the action. There were "lumpens" who snuck into the FALPO's ranks because it meant they could "live off of the movement."

Marino was as grimy as they came. He had the phraseology and posture of a revolutionary. That was it. He was a criminal element passing as an organizer. The CC kept him at a safe distance, never fully trusting him.

Marino was in charge of organizing factory workers in different parts of the Bronx. He ran "number games," charging interest to loan Dominican immigrant workers money. He used his union position to promise vulnerable, minimum-wage workers he could get them raises and union positions if they slept with him. He showed up late at night when other party men were working — carrying out political responsibilities— and proposed sex for money to their wives or partners. Claiming he understood how tough times were economically for the women —because of their sacrifices alongside good party men— he said he wouldn't tell anyone if they took a few hundred bucks from him.

The rank-and-file of the MPD sniffed out the *lumpen* behavior and pushed for an investigation and an internal trial. They found Marino guilty and he was immediately stripped of every responsibility. Instead of facing the truth with integrity, he went on the run. There was a proposal to put a bullet in his head. Others suggested breaking his two legs. At the end of it all, what was Marino but a pathetic representation of this contemptable world which produces opportunists and rats? He received a pass and became a bus driver in District 7 of the Bronx, never to cross paths with the movement again.

NGO's: Neoliberal Government Organizations

To understand Orlando's personality and predicament, the reader has to comprehend the MPD's relationship with the world of charity. The MPD rejected the Non-Governmental Organization model which they referred to as Neoliberal Government Organizations. This decision was not because the staff of the NGO's, the Peace Core and their missionary counterparts were bad people, per se. From the perspective of the centralized party, the problem was that NGO's did the reformist work that the revolutionary forces were better equipped to do. Who was better situated to rebuild after natural disasters than an anti-imperialist grass roots movement that was rooted in the affected communities?

Well-meaning Americans give to charities every day. But by funding organizations —such as the Red Cross, OXFAM, USAID and other outfits in cahoots with the U.S. State Department — they buttress imperialism.

The point of reformist work was to wage small, local struggles while advancing the greater cause of exposing and overthrowing the entire dominant paradigm. Immediate gains like unionization or the formation of a neighborhood organization — which mobilizes for a new sewerage system— were important but they were not the end goal. Liberalism —shallow and short-sighted—never dared to go beyond the achievement of crumbs. The MPD rejected the idea of "negotiating the terms of exploitation" because it sought to overthrow the entire boss/wage slave and oppressor nation/oppressed nation relationship.[34]

The ruling circles —the most class conscious of actors— understood this dynamic and diverted resources elsewhere for public relations purposes. Through tockenism, they highlighted "development" work and projected the image of the altruistic, benefactor state. A tally of the amount of "development" workers in a nation existed in direct proportion to how oppressed that nation was. Haiti and the nations of Southern Africa are among the nations with the highest amount of "do-gooders" in proportion to their populations. How are those "developing nations" faring? Has any of that "charity" achieved anything beyond some momentary relief for oppressed individuals and jobs for foreign "humanitarian-workers?" Charity is the left hand of the state. The right hand is the repression of the liberation movement.

Exposure of the NGO's true function was part of Marxist training but Orlando saw things his own way. Orlando stood 6' 2 and weighed a slender and strong 185 lbs. Gregarious and unassuming, he built rapport with everybody.[35] One day he socialized with nuns; the next day with students from elite colleges. He was a people person with no limits. According to Orlando's view of the world, there were no enemies. That was just who he was.

---

[34] Quote from Vladimir Lenin in <u>What is to Be Done?</u>
[35] In movement parlance, it was common to simply say "Orlando built with everybody," meaning he built positive relationships and camaraderie that sought to strengthen the movement.

Leadership continually warned him that he could not represent both the FALPO and foreign-run NGOs, who pushed an agenda at odds with that of the party. After the third warning, the Central Committee suspended him for collaborating with an NGO and entertaining the idea of taking a job with them. The verdict on Orlando was that he was a great friend and person but he was ideologically weak. The Central Committee consistently and patiently reasoned with him to stay away from the NGO world but in the dialectic of the "carrot and stick approach," the carrot won out.

From the perspective of imperialism, the idea of independent, grassroots organizations restoring —not just infrastructure, but dignity and self-determination— was too risky. The ruling class destroyed the revolutionary forces with one hand and threw the dispossessed pitiful handouts with the other. The neo-colonizing state masqueraded as a welfare state that selflessly did what it could through humanitarian aid to help the poor nations of the Caribbean, while it extracted resources and surplus value at will.

President Barack Obama had the gall to exalt the U.S.'s grandiose nature in his latest State of the Union address. In offering his rationale for the latest round of bombings on the Middle East, he remarked "When Haiti or the Philippines is in trouble, who swoops in to help them?"[36] Appealing to American's innate sense of good and wrong, the current CEO of U.S. capitalism has very effectively shored up more confidence in the U.S. than Bush Sr. or Jr. ever could.

Paternalism, white supremacy and a "1st world needs to help the 3rd world" attitude pervaded the NGO's. Humanitarian and charity workers were detached from reality and history. If their work had any truly profound effect on society, it too would be declared illegal. Charity workers could begin to un-learn by picking up some books about Dominican, Latin American and African history. Eduardo Galeano's The Open Veins of Latin America: Five Centuries of the Pillage of a Continent —which Hugo Chavez famously gave to Barack Obama at the UN— is one place to start.

---

[36] State of the Union address January 20, 2015.

Understand, in the Caribbean, there are no poor countries. There are only exploited countries. This truly is an upside down world. The MPD had full confidence that this could be rectified and human relations could be catapulted to another dimension.

Buying off Talent

Orlando's wife, Kiki, earned $6,000 pesos every two weeks stitching undergarments for Fruit of a Loom, Hanes and other U.S. brand name companies. That was the equivalent of US$71 for 55 hour work weeks. Who could live and raise a family on this salary? What young person would resist the temptation of transnational migration and voluntarily choose to enslave themselves for their entire lives, for a mere pittance? What intelligent father would not pursue an opening within the NGO world?

The one armed bandit that Walter Rodney identified in <u>How Europe Underdeveloped Africa</u> pillaged with one hand and distributed some pacifying crumbs with the other. These illusion-bearing organizations did nothing to forward justice in exploited countries and existed in fact to retard it. Orlando claimed he understood the position of maintaining distance from the NGOs but the lure of some proximity to white, visa-carrying Westerners and a dignified salary was too strong. Like many potential organic intellectuals —who might have been guided by an anti-imperialist world outlook and worked on behalf of the poor— Orlando was bought off. He accepted a position in the periphery of an NGO that worked under the auspices of the U.S. Agency of International Development. He rose in the ranks of their NGO until he became the national director and received a visa to travel back and forth to the US. He then solicited his wife and daughter to join him in the land of ~~opportunity~~ stolen riches. Imperialist funds indirectly bought off talent and *dirigentes*.[37] This was by design.

---

[37] For more information on this topic see Petras, James. "NGO's: In the Service of Imperialism." *Journal of Contemporary Asia*. Volume: 29. Issue: 4. Publication Year: 1999. Page Number: 429.

The Gate and Bridge Keepers

Caridad was a force to be reckoned with. She was fond of gunplay and violence. No one called her by her first name. So fortified was her reputation as a rebel, she was simply known as "*la quema-goma*," "the tire-burner."

This is the story of how she emerged as one of the top lieutenants of the FALPO.

Caridad grew up a downtrodden, battered *campesina* (peasant girl) in the *campo* (the countryside). During local uprisings, she covered her face and stood watch on a bridge and charged chauffeurs a toll to drive their vehicle by. She laid giant branches across the key roads and lit tires on fire in order to demand her toll. Extorting the meager resources of the innocent, and sometimes not so innocent, was her trade. The *voceros* approached the RobinHood like character and her gang of ruffians. They partially admired how she commanded the area with the band of hirelings who answered to her; she just needed direction and a step back from her immediate, demeaning reality of poverty, they thought.

The FALPO approached her to explain the difference between common criminals and revolutionaries, individualists and collectivists. She shrugged them off and told them "vete a la mierda" ("Go &^$# yourself)". Another delegation returned seven days later with an ultimatum: "You fuck with us or we're gonna fuck with you."[38] Backed up against the wall and left with no real choice, she entered into an alliance with the party.

There were those pacifists who took offense to the strategies of intimidation and force that were employed to enroll Caridad in the people's army. But who were these sideline quarterbacks to judge? There was nothing peaceful about unemployment, hunger and poverty. How could Caridad project non-violence when everything around her reeked of destruction and relegated her community to an early, demeaning death?

---

[38] Slang for you work with us or we will regard you as an enemy and take you out of the highway business.

Not even the revolutionary optimists could predict that Caridad would adopt a broader world view so quickly and see beyond the immediate deprivation and needs of her family. She, who was a highway bandit, now enforced the law of revolution. She renounced her former highway skullduggery and funneled all of her skills and fearlessness into a new outlet.

"Not on my watch"

When Caridad caught someone hustling on the people's watch, she gave them a warning. The second time, she put a gun to their knees. She remarked: "It's never personal. But you *tigueres* (gangsters) make all of us all look bad. They already talk one hundred percent negative about the FALPO in the media. Why give them more ammunition? If they are not with us, they are working against us. We can't have this." She who had outrun revolutionary morality, now enforced revolutionary justice.

Being a young woman leader in a predominately male space only toughened Caridad's resolve and decreased her appetite for nonsense and abuse. When a male ally and "mentor" took advantage of a late night work session to try to touch her inappropriately, she withdrew her pistol. She pressed her compact Glock 19 to his right eye, asking him if he still wanted some action.

Quick to draw a gun out of the back of her pants, she sought to discipline two young FALPistas on another occasion for disrespecting a group of women. In the commotion her pistol accidently went off, striking herself in the arm and one of the young men in the shoulder. The leadership disciplined her but did not even consider taking her coveted firearm.. The FALPO didn't want the wildcard "quema-goma" on the loose again.

Overcoming Poverty and Patriarchy

Caridad emerged as a loyal partywoman in the isolated, dirt roads of Pontoncito. She guided a group of young leaders in training from La Capital through her village. There were small children gathering atop a giant *basurero* (trash dump), striking down the *ciguas* (small palmchat birds), hovering over the garbage with slingshots. They scooped up expired cans of tomato sauce and brought these birds home to their families to fry up for dinner. Some of the leaders from urban backgrounds had never seen this rung of the social inferno. They later remarked that visiting Caridad was their second baptism into el MPD.

Caridad was the first in her family to graduate from high school. Too poor to scrounge up the change for the public bus, every morning she walked for over an hour to get to school. She had escaped a level of insidiousness difficult for an outsider to imagine. Caridad was a survivor of horrific abuse. Her grandmother was married for many years with her first husband and had eight children. She left this abusive relationship and remarried. Her grandmother's new husband raped her daughters. Caridad's mom, Maribel was 13-years-old when she got pregnant with Caridad. Caridad told how her mother beat her own belly senseless, trying to kill Caridad before she could be conceived. It was traumatizing stories like these that were all too common for women battling the twin evils of poverty and machismo. Caridad was the perfect synthesis of this profound insidiousness and the rebellion to which it gave birth. Those who had survived and emerged from the backwater hellhole, were the only ones capable of vanquishing it.

Caridad and her family poured forth testimonies of incest, wonton sexual abuse of children, alcoholism, the battering of women, and machete brawls that left teenagers without limbs. These stories were usually hushed up and considered to be shameful for the family. With the newfound support, the floodgates of her pain opened up. Her cousins and nieces —thirteen year old girls who had not yet reached puberty— were already veterans of hustling and sex work. Their environs had left them no other option.

AIDS had devastated Caridad's family, claiming her mother and three of her siblings. At her sister's wedding, their sickly mother's last wish was to dance with her new son-in-law. But she was in too much pain because of an opportunistic infection called *culebria* or "the disease of the snake," so named because of how it wrapped around the victims' stomach. A local legend circulated that when the infection completed its course around a person's midsection, the victim died. *Culebria* was the rural vernacular for the opportunistic infection known as "shingles," which had penetrated her nerves. Three months later, Caridad's mother died in complete agony.

In 2004, there were funerals every week for Caridad's family members who became infected with the virus. For nine days and nights, the village remembered the deceased, gathering together over drink and food. The neighborhood alcoholics appeared out of nowhere to supposedly "fulfill" their familial obligation but everyone knew their true motives, to score a free meal and bottle of rum. Close woman relatives, more pious than the rest, took vows not to go to parties, nor anywhere they would be "enjoying" themselves and to wear only black clothes.   Sometimes this mourning lasted for years.

There were times when one wake overlapped with another.   The opportunist village supermarket owner, and hunger pains, coerced another one of Caridad's sisters to sleep with him so she and her three young children didn't starve.   She too contracted the virus.

Caridad's family was big.   One night, she wrote out the names of all of her sisters and brothers.   She read off the list of her own siblings, checking it several times before remembering a member of the family tree she had left out.   "Our lives are not worth a rotten *guanabana* (soursop)," she exclaimed.   She was right.   Who in the entire world was taking note of who lived or died in this tiny, isolated village outside of Mao Valverde?   Only when the living deceased rose up from their zombified state of being did the state notice that they existed.   In the words of Caridad: "We tried to wake them up with our words and tears, but they only hear us when we spew bullets."

To have a key cadre of the movement embedded in this type of suffering meant Caridad needed extra support —emotionally and ideologically— but it is also meant she would never turn back.   Her impulse was to pump lead into any problem she came across.   She had emerged from Pontoncito, the swamps of hell and she had no intention of going back.   For the first time, lined up shoulder to shoulder with her comrades, she tasted a freedom that assured her that life did not have to be synonymous with humiliation.

Precisely because she had cleaned up her act, commanded the loyalty of a type of outlaw gang and could no longer be bought off, Caridad now became a real target of the military.

In 2008, after a three day strike that shut down the province, la quema-goma attempted to return to her village.   As she drove her moped home late at night, undercover military operatives chased her down in pick-up trucks.   They rammed her small bike off of the road and it crashed into the darkness twenty feet underneath a bridge.   Seeing that she was alive, grasping for life, the stage agents pursued her and delivered the execution-style *"tiro de gracia."*[39] The other MPD loyalist, Fausto —afraid he would suffer a similar fate— hurled himself into the raging waters below. Unable to swim amidst the mighty currents, he too passed on to sainthood.

Ten years later, Caridad's legacy has only grown. The teenage warriors, who belong to this generation of fighters, train in the spirit of Caridad.

"Pigs" versus Human Beings

The police in an oppressed country are unlike the police in the belly of the beast. Their class character is radically different. In DR, the average policeman earns less than a $100 per month for fifty hours of "service" each week. There were interactions that revealed the humility of individual police officers.

Every year, the MPD organized a photography exhibit that documented five decades of martyrdom. They sent representatives to travel around the country teaching this untold history. The exhibit consisted of hundreds of portraits and artifacts that documented the party's courageous and sanguinary history. Universities and public plazas hosted the display which functioned as a recruiting tool and an antidote to half-truths spouted out by the media.

The party sent representatives to travel around the country with the exhibition. One night in 2001, four cadre stayed up all night in a public plaza of San Pedro de Macoris to watch over the exhibit. Sharing pieces of bread with salami and cheese, they rotated who slept and who was on lookout. Their guard was always up. A police patrol came towards them in an unthreatening way. Two young officers aimlessly sauntered around the park, their gazes wandering far off into the night. They had hunger and humanity in their eyes.

---

[39] A final bullet delivered to someone's head who is already injured and defenseless.

The MPD youth called the two officers over and offered them some morsels of food. Without uttering a word, they graciously smiled and accepted. Under different political circumstances, they may have sat down to break bread, but they had surprise and fear in their eyes. How would they explain to their bosses that they were fraternizing with the "enemy?" This natural moment of bonding with the police would never happen in Missouri or California. Impossible. The police in an oppressor country identify with the class that they protect and kill for. In the periphery, real alliances can be built with individual members of the police.

The movement calls the police in the U.S. "pigs" because they act like pigs, arrogantly patrolling and occupying communities that they are at war with. The term "pig" was first coined by Huey P. Newton —Minister of Defense and propagandist of the Black Panther Party— to capture the vile nature of the state. When in the history of the U.S. have the police allied with the oppressed? They have always been the persecutors and executioners of the resistance fighters. Since the slavocracy first recruited police officers as slave hunters, they were employed to keep the oppressed in check.

But these teenage police officers —uprooted from their villages halfway across the country— were not pigs. They joined the ranks of the state to help their families. Their pathetically low wages prevented their families from starving, but did not achieve much more than that.

The military represents a different class segment of the population. The day will come in the U.S. —as it does in every revolution— when the military turns their guns on the police. In the Dominican Republic the class character of the police was different. Both the police and the military were drawn from the bottom rungs of society. The FALPO membership often had sisters or brothers in the police. Granted, in most moments of naked class strife —these "sisters and brothers" followed the orders of their commanding officers and fired bullets at el FALPO. But there were also moments that rekindled the hope of winning over sections of the state to defend their own class interests. Though this may sound surreal to the American-based audience, there were times when friends and family members who were "police officers" saved the lives of the FALPO leadership.

Understanding this dynamic, the party sent teenage cadre into the military and police to infiltrate their ranks in order to have eyes and ears within the state. These contacts tipped the FALPO off so that they knew who the police were gunning for and when they would strike. This tactic saved many innocent lives, as we shall learn later in our story.

Los Guaricanos[40]

Javier, nicknamed "El Gallo," and Wendy worked in the Secretariat of the MPD.[41] They oversaw the day to day activities in an impoverished neighborhood of Villa Mella. On Friday nights, the members prepared a collective feast. Someone brought the *moro (rice and beans cooked together)*, someone else the *lechón* (marinated pig meat) and someone the wine. They studied the lyrics of Latin America's greatest poets, Silvio Rodriguez, Mercedes "La Negra" Sosa and Pablo Milanés, taking turns looking up words and interpreting the imagery and metaphors present in the lyrics. Guests from revolutionary movements from Colombia, Libya, the DPRK and around the world made appearances and walked through the pitch-black candle lit alleyways to visit and exchange ideas and experiences. No small, flimsy, plastic cup of wine ever tasted so divine.

Javier's cousin, Junior joined the police out of necessity. He had no genuine loyalty to the state but rather needed a paycheck to support his family. His training and time in the barracks had not solidified any false loyalties or fake patriotism as it does in the academy of the NYPD. In or out of his uniform, Junior was at one with the masses. This would prove to be a determining factor of great importance.

---

[40] Notorious ghetto at the entrance of Villa Mella, Santo Domingo.
[41] Secretariat is another name for the Central Committee of the MPD.

The FALPO organized a getaway one Sunday for marginalized youth to escape the shantytowns and partake in an afternoon at a river and waterfall. The bus trip was over an hour long as it cut through the mountains of San Cristobal. Everyone enjoyed themselves and the first half of the trip was without incident. On the way back, many youth had drank too much. As the bachata blared out across the bus, the youth in the back became more raucous and reckless. Among them were bona fide, heartless and brainless dope-dealers and gang bangers, the social products of a heartless system. A few of them had done time in prison and had been involved in street warfare that left others injured and dead. The FALPO sought a truce with them, meaning "you all do your thing, we will do ours," but was not naïve about who they were and what they were capable of.

Not too far from home, one of the gang's chiefs, El Rubio (Blondie), harassed one of Javier's cousins named Marisol. When she rejected his advances, he slapped her. No one knew what had happened, until she timidly showed Javier her bruised eye. Javier immediately pursued El Rubio with the intent of putting him in his place. Javier spun him around prepared to unload a series of punches. El Rubio and his crew pulled out knives and the FALPO leaders were forced to retreat. *Los lumpenes* (the lumpen elements) had had the last word for that particular day.[42]

That night the FALPO's local leadership congregated at Javier's house plotting the next night's offering of justice. The following night the people's sentence would be delivered: two broken legs and a minimum of one month in the hospital. The national spokesperson from the CC, a veteran from the *La Guerra de Abril* (the War of April), El Men, who chaired the meeting, explained that when you strike, you strike hard so that your nemeses cannot contemplate exacting revenge: "By the time they regain consciousness, their only desire would be to live and their desire to avenge their beating would be diminished."

---

[42] The lumpen proletariat is a Marxist term for the most oppressed, unemployed layers of society, cast into the world of hustling to survive.

They summoned FALPistas who were martial arts experts, two drivers, and another carload for backup. As the moon rose up over the zinc shacks of Villa Milla, El Rubio and his crew smoked weed on a corner. The peoples' vigilantes arrived on the scene and surrounded them. Those in charge of grabbing his legs and containing him became entangled with his cohorts and fell down in pursuit of him. Though the FALPO delegation delivered some shots with baseball bats, El Rubio escaped relatively unscathed.

The delegation regrouped back at Javier's home, a few hundred meters from where the drama had unfolded. They kept a look out at all times in front of the house and the night went by calmly, as they pondered what the next night would bring. The serenity of the night foreboded a potential nightmare.

The next night a fresh, serene breeze circulated the neighborhood. All of the sudden, gunshots and screams burst through the air. A crowd of one hundred counter-vigilantes congregated as a lynch mob. With blood in their eyes, they sought revenge against El FALPO. El Rubio had mobilized his entire neighborhood against the revolutionary organization, depicting the FALPO as the bullies and aggressors. In the propaganda war, he had won. The Guaricanos had turned against the very forces who defended them. Grandmothers, middle age women and even younger middle school kids grasped rocks, machetes and whatever else could be unleashed against el FALPO. They shot Javier's house up. Fortunately, the FALPO entourage were armed and Junior, the aforementioned police officer, was visiting and happened to be in the house. It was only their return fire that kept the crowd at bay.

Cellular phones were a novelty in early 2001. Luckily, the boxed-in MPD leaders had access to one. They called the national coordinator of El FALPO, whispering to him through the phone and articulating the gravity of the situation. Reinforcements were sent in and arrived within twenty minutes. Mostly warming shots were fired above the heads of the crowd. El FALPO did not want to draw blood from its own class. They preferred to live to fight another day, temporarily retreating to gather more momentum. Through jagged, narrow alleyways in the back of the neighborhood, the FALPO's outside support whisked away the Guaricanos' local leadership. As they sped off, they saw blood splattered up and down the dirt alleyways and lumpen youth gathered ready for round two of the war. They did not look back. They had survived to fight another day.

The Guaricanos leadership left all of their personal possessions behind. Two months passed before they reestablished a truce with the local gang and returned to collect what was left of their clothes and furniture. The lumpens burnt Javier's home to a crisp. Three generations of his family were forced to relocate. Javier had to teach the next morning. It was clear that he was wearing clothes several sizes too small for him. How surreal to be in front of a group of high school kids, so soon after having been in the middle of a shootout that almost ended in death. That was a long night, one that everyone was fortunate to have survived. It was a testament to the FALPO's discipline that a half dozen *"lumpen"* youth were not killed by revolutionary bullets. The watchwords: *Viscous before the enemy, Humble before the people* was the code they lived by.

A meeting of dirigentes in Salcedo.

Navarrete: Tierra Caliente[43]

Navarrete's reputation preceded it everywhere one travelled in the Dominican Republic. A random passenger in the Santiago airport –upon overhearing that a fellow traveler was headed south to Navarrete— warned everyone to watch out for the FALPistas who stopped passing vehicles, with burning tires and mugged the passengers. If he only knew that those "terrorists and thugs" were the protection and the future salvation of this imperialist-damned land. He was shaped by the press to believe that socialist fighters — derogatorily referred to as "stone-throwers and tire-burners"— were mindless "hood rats" who had nothing better to do than terrorize the "peaceful" order of things.

The Dominican Republic —like all former Spanish colonies— is deeply Catholic. During Christmas time, Victor and another *dirigente* were called upon to give a toast. Felix forgot that this was a depoliticized family, sympathetic to the FALPO through familial relations. In his toast, he jumped directly into urging the families gathered there to "gear up for struggle and to never surrender in the new year." He fell back on political rhetoric without properly reading his surroundings. The hosts thought nothing of it, but a MPD leader, Victor, cordially and privately critiqued Felix later that night: "*Compañero,* you did not extend gratitude to the people's homes we are in. You were caught up in the struggle and forgot the simple things that we cannot afford to forget."

This was a valuable lesson for revolutionaries to carry with them. In the revolutionary fervor don't forget the simple things, like expressing gratitude and having manners. The FALPO trained their young militants to pay close attention to the Catholic and *campesino* (rural) idiosyncrasies of the people. This can go a long way in terms of earning the respect of the people, the immense sea in which revolutionaries swim. It is these very families that will hide *dirigentes* when the military pursues them or smuggle them a plate of *moro con pescado* (rice, beans and fish), when they are hungry.

---

[43] Navarrete: Scorching Hot Land in reference to this town being the hotbed of revolutionary activity.

With out the support and trust of the local population, a revolutionary is a fish out of water.

"I confess. I have lived."

I walked the streets with the organizer of the organizers, the captain of the captains. Victor trained an entire generation of hotheads. Families and an eclectic group of young men with intentions, both survival-minded and opportunistic, invaded *solares*,[44] they wished to build homes on. They were taking the land back from an absentee land owner who lived in Spain. Even though some leaders vouched for me, some peasant families did not recognize me and did not approve of me being there. The rumor mill was in full swing: "Is he a Mormon? Everyone knows the Mormons are CIA agents. Is he filming us? Is he mapping out the winding alley passageways to get here?" My fellow countrymen almost always arrive in foreign lands —if they arrive at all— as missionaries, tourists or charity workers. Convinced as they are of the need for yet another round of "manifest destiny," they urge far-away peoples, in far-flung places, to see the world through the prism of their religion. Have the missionaries ever stopped to think how they would feel if the evangelicals of other lands invaded their neighborhoods and ways of life to convince them of another spiritual view? Arrogance continues to be the medium that characterizes North-South relations.

Danito was the head of the unorganized, lawless elements. The tall, intimidating man with bronze, chiseled muscles and a baritone voice came towards me: "What's in the backpack?" He ripped the backpack open and my notebook and poems scattered everywhere. An argument ensued about whether to let me stay or not. It was anarchy. It led to other arguments about which plot of land belong to whom. The more well off speculators hired poor families to squat on a plot so that they could then buy the deed off of them. Suddenly, there were gunshots back and forth. I was again in over my head. I needed to get out of there. Victor was the only one

---

[44] parceled out plots of land

from our organization on the scene. He was waiting for other FALPistas to fortify their position for the pending police attacks. Amidst the gunshots, he made himself heard and vouched for me: "Anything happens to this big fella, you'll have a problem with us. He's one of us. He's with the FALPO."

I was amazed at how one man's intervention could completely calm the situation. It reminded me of the control Malcolm X exercised in Harlem after a Black motorist was brutalized by the police. The angry crowd that had gathered took their cues from Malcolm. With simple motions of his hands or curt commands, Victor controlled the situation.

It was a Saturday morning twelve years later. We were visiting the homes and families of as many of the young slain revolutionaries that we could before lunch. This was Victor's monthly routine, to make sure everyone was taken care of. The FALPO's loyalty was reminiscent of Sicily's mafia: you taking care of your own. Within a twenty five block radius, we visited nine families who lost their children to state terrorism. Every time I shook the hands or embraced the proud parents, grandparents and orphans of fallen FALPistas, I was seized by a potent combination of tragedy, anger and pride. They spoke of the dead as though they were still here, up to their old antics, giving the rich hell, and standing up for the rights of the dispossessed. Because I was a friend and mentor to their sons, I too was looked upon as family. There were more smiles of pride than tears of agony, just as the slain saints would have wanted.

We visited other burn victims which made me remember el Líder Quibio. Samson, who was half Haitian and half Dominican, and El Bacán, who was the father of five, were experts in preparing homemade explosives. The people's greatest self-defense was their offense. Molotov cocktails kept the police a safe distance away, but in the preparation of the defensive weapons, these two patriots suffered accidents when the homemade bombs exploded in their hands. All of the limbs and lives lost, should be put squarely on the shoulders of the status-quo who indifferently maintain an inexplicable economic and social design.

Victor limped down the street a piece of shrapnel from the police still lodged into his lower back. A martial arts expert, he was never able to continue his training after being shot when he was sixteen by a police bullet. He never stayed in the same house more than one night. The *compañeros* slept in shifts, making sure someone was always on duty, in case the police showed up to haul someone off or open up fire on the sleeping. As we left the house of the late Hipólito, a younger warrior asked him, "Brother it must feel weird sometimes. There are too many dead. They were all like your younger brothers. How were you able to come home from war?" Solemn and more determined than ever, he responded, "What can I say? In the words of Gabriel Garcia Marquez, 'I confess I have lived.'"

Elvis "Oni" Rodiguez, one of the saints...RIP

The Prodigal Son

Just this past month, I returned to the Dominican Republic to assist in our latest campaigns and remain up to date with the FALPO's work. I brought my son 12-year-old Ernesto Rafael with me. His mother is from a notoriously active hotbed of revolutionary ferment, the town of Tamboril. She always cautioned me about bringing him with me because of the potential danger. I wanted him to begin to comprehend the class struggle that was playing out in his homeland. It was also important for him to practice his Spanish by staying and interacting with his cousins and extended family. I knew he had a passion for rock-throwing after our stint in Belfast staying with Éirígí, the Irish resistance, but logically his mother was worried sick that he would follow his father's insurrectionary footsteps. I wanted him to absorb the experience, but alas, how could I forgive myself if something ever happened to him?

On a Wednesday, the government announced they were moving one of the FALPO's political prisoners, Adonai, from one prison to another, hours further away from his hometown of Tamboril. The next evening the city exploded into rebellion. The evening of the strike, I left Ernesto behind in neutral territory with his aunt and cousins. I wanted him to see how his community came together in the streets but I was afraid of the risks.

I was back in familiar territory. The mobilization charged forward, chanting in unison:

> *"Caldero vacio*
> *Aqui va a ver un lio*
> *Sin agua sin luz*
> *Aqui va a ver un rebu"*[45]

People's arms were interlocked. The crowd swelled. The chant leaders bounced up and down and the crowd followed. The march was reminiscent of the *toyi-toyi* national dance of the Zimbabwean and South Africa freedom fighters when they rose up against apartheid.[46] The rearguard surged forth with a line of tires soaked in gasoline. *Puuffffff.* In the blaze of flames, the class lines were drawn. The police could no longer advance towards the crowd.

---

[45] "Empty pots Here watch us riot. Without water without electricity here comes the revolt."

[46] https://www.youtube.com/watch?v=u5OfDFK1yyU&list=PLpxF5MKoO5jnyHTIWo mk0qcV7Dyi2eB9n

Flish flash shu shu. Dozens of rocks sent the police barricade scattering. *Uff Uff.* Tear gas canisters dispersed the crowd. Everyone ran for their lives. Balaclava-clad youth returned the tear gas canisters sending the police scattering in the four directions. They fired live ammunition. A thirteen-year-old kid, following and imitating his older brother, was hit. I thought of my own son. The entire *Sanchez* —one of the most infamous *barrios* in the country with its reputation for militancy— was mobilized. The military police controlled the main street that cuts through Tamboril, but they were on a foreign battlefield that would soon collapse in on them. They fired off hundreds of rounds into the homes where the FALPistas hid. Shots were fired back. A low ranking officer was hit in the leg. The underpaid poor devils pursued the insurgent youth house to house. At one point, there were four simultaneous shootouts taking place at once. The people had the last say and the military police were overwhelmed, more concerned with surviving the night than beating the unbeatable community. The police were on the run. They were forced out of Tamboril, but not before leaving behind a fresh set of martyrs. Two blocks away from his house, Junior laid lifeless, his body strewn across the asphalt for his mother and aunt to pick up. They pleaded with God to restore life to his sinewy body. But the prayers of the poor have never been an equal match for the weapons of the rich. Another innocent child of the hardship was stolen from their side. That night I hugged my son and tucked him into bed like I do every night. I tried to share some parts of what had happened only hours earlier so that he could understand that his people were under attack on both sides of the Caribbean Sea. He told me about how much fun he had with his cousins at a local pool. I thought, isn't that how it should be for all of the children of this defiant, divine people?

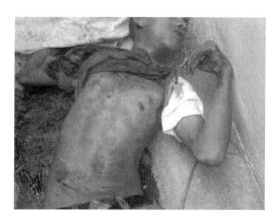

Youth, sacrificed

The Student Leader who Sold Out for a *Chele*[47]

Jenuel was a *vocero* of a different breed. He bragged about the power he had as a student leader and how he shut down entire high-schools with a few commands. He boasted about cheating on exams to pass his courses because the teachers were powerless to stop him. The boisterous and plump Jenuel was more interested in gunplay and bravado than diligently fulfilling the tasks of his highly-respected position. He was not a "quiof the people," he was a laggard, a braggart and an opportunist.

"A tribune of the people" is a concept the Russian revolutionary, Vladimir Lenin explored in his ground-breaking 1905 pamphlet What is to be Done? Lenin outlined how a revolutionary leader should be able to respond to all manifestations of inequality and patiently explain to the workers that all injustice stems from a common origin, the capitalist system. The MPD youth studied Lenin, Mao, Rosa Luxemburg, Ernesto Che Guevara, Maximiliano Gomez and other past "tribunes of the people" and sought to emulate their examples.

Jenuel despised study. He was the diametrical opposite of Lenin's "tribune" and should have never been allowed to ascend to

---

[47] A dollar.

such a position. His actions and careerism were used to discredit the integrity of the entire movement. He and his running mates took new recruits on a tour of his neighborhood, Cristo Rey. He then invited everyone to a strip club. Like a corpulent seal, belly-up, basking under the sun, he felt at home in this sleazy, humiliating scene. With embezzled funds, he bought rounds of drinks and ordered lap dances. One round led to another and then young woman danced nude on a stage, giving lap dances to the inebriated clientele. The bourgeoisie preferred a "leader" like Jenuel that they could wheel and deal with. Jenuel had a price and his overseers knew exactly how much it was. Lenin looked on, repulsed, rolling in his grave, issuing directives that this opportunist be unseated from his throne of power and influence, immediately.

At four a.m. the crew spilled onto the main boulevard of Cristo Rey, wound up and laughing. The bachata of Zacarias Ferreira blared out over the streets which reeked of piss and depravity. A stench of sewage and fried fast food permeated the night. Alcoholics, addicts and the police were on the prowl, sizing each other up, competing for the next victim they could shake down. There was a line for the *chimichuri* (hamburger) cart and a line of men of all ages who chugged their last beers of the *madrugada* (early morning) while gobbling down *fritura*.[48] Jenuel's henchmen were so full and bloated, they swore they were going to burst. Across the street, a dozen sex workers waved down cars in hopes of finding a paying client. The decrepit images and the smell and sight of garbage everywhere was nauseating. This was a telling snapshot of what globalization means for Dominican society. Dreams and visions of what could be were drowned out in the rum and misogyny. To accept such a harrowing reality was never an option. Before the anguish, El MPD's tribunes asked: "Where is the dignity? Where is the pride? We are the children of Lemba, Santiago Basora, Francisco del Rosario Sánchez, las hermanas Mirabal and Caamaño. How can we stay silent?"

Within two years Jenuel had "flipped" and was a state spy. The movement placed a bounty on his head. He rose up in the ranks

---

[48] Deep-fried pieces of pork.

of the elite summits of power and joined one of the two ruling class parties, the misnamed Dominican Revolutionary Party (PRD), climbing their ranks to become the coordinator of their national security. He now lived in a plush, fully furnished apartment on John F. Kennedy Boulevard, far away from his humble roots. He had a servant and driver and he spoke to them with that imperious tone of someone who had servants and drivers his entire life.

In a shootout between old running mates, Jenuel and his bodyguards injured three FALPistas, one fatally. Juanchinchin and Snyder were forced to go into hiding. Jenuel skipped town. He resurfaced eight months later when he assumed everything was safe. But the MPD had a long memory and was not about to let bygones be bygones. The FALPO's beef with snitches was parallel to the CRIP and BLOOD war that ravaged South Central LA in the 1980's. The two entities refused to coexist. On a moist Friday night, Jenuel returned to his old stomping grounds in La 70 of Cristo Rey. In front of his black, bullet-proof SUV, bought with state funds, he threw back *Presidentes,* the national beer, and played dominos, as the salsa roared out into the night. Two mopeds sped up towards him. The FALPO drivers looked forward. Two gunmen, who were strapped to the drivers' backs, sat facing backward. Without helmets, a disguise or protection, the shooters shouted taunts at the beer-bellied big talker. Jenuel was sent off to another world before his drinking buddies could make sense of what was transpiring. His blood splattered over the dominoes table and into the dirt. Before his bodyguards could fire back, the fleeing mopeds had skirted down an adjacent alleyway. Unfortunately, the only language Jenuel spoke was the language of lead.

"I am First and Foremost, a Professional Revolutionary"

A doctor, Idelsa arrived behind enemy lines one day because she agreed to tend to two gunshot victims, Juanchinchin and Snyder, without asking any questions. She was a new contact the foot soldiers met as she did fieldwork in an adjacent village for Haitian-Dominican children born without birth certificates, citizenship, a national flag or a homeland. Born into a more privileged reality, she never imagined treating somebody from the notorious FALPO. It was her first interaction with the ill-famed *"bandidos"* (criminals). The news had so thoroughly dehumanized the FALPistas that at first she was hesitant to enter into an abysmally poor village on the outskirts of Monticristi to attend to them. Prodded on by the Hippocratic Oath, she entered a dirt-floor hovel to examine Juanchinchin.

Idelsa was dressed immaculately, with her brunette hair carefully propped up. It was as if the humid weather had no effect on her. The fallen patient stared in awe at her bouncing dark hair, delicate frame and perfectly bronzed skin. It appeared as though her flowing beauty took away some of the pain of Juanchinchin's internal bleeding.

Idelsa organically formed bonds with the poverty-stricken, underground rebels and this changed her forever. She became the FALPO's clandestine doctor. Already equipped with years of education, she began to study Marxism and master the sweet science of social change. Gradually she turned her back on the old world and embraced her new family. Idelsa participated in study groups and oriented young recruits on how to fulfill membership requirements. The extreme polarization of society had radicalized her. She reasoned that if capitalism called into existence two separate poles —one of misery, the other of luxury— she was duty-bound to stand with the former.

The people's doctor lived a dual life. No one from her circle of friends, at the expensive Catholic University PUCMM (pronounced Pu-ka-mai-ma), imagined she had anything to do with the infamous FALPO. Accustomed to abundance, she never showed up empty-handed to evaluate a wounded warrior. She expropriated and liberated resources from her affluent milieu and the well-stocked university and turned them over to the party. She risked everything because she was touched by the vision of the young warriors.

As was inevitable, many a young soldier's heart was afflicted by their admiration and school boy, dream-like fantasies of Idelsa. She maintained the most serious demeanor, never allowing any of the spellbound lads to cross the line with her. She reiterated to a generation of young men, raised in a *machista* society, lacking strong revolutionary women mentors, that she was first and foremost a professional revolutionary. She contrasted the word professional with amateur for clarification. She said an amateur doctor would be working for the corrupt government of President Hipólito Mejía, dedicated solely to building up their own bank account.

First and foremost, a revolutionary.

Fifteen years later, Idelsa still believes in and supports the national liberation movement. A diagnostician of the individual and social body, she leads cadre schools and develops curricula around simplifying the core Marxist and Maoist concepts of alienation, surplus value, the vanguard, the mass line, people's war and national liberation. She explained that her life was a testament to the movement watchwords: "Everyone, revolutionary or otherwise, has a role to play."[49] Her *machista* society inquired everyday why she never married or had children. She explained that she *was* married

[49] Quote adopted from the words of Irish Republican political prisoner, Bobby Sands.

to the struggle and had more children than they could ever imagine, and that furthermore, she had nothing to explain to anyone. She lived life on her own terms.

The naysayers submit that "they don't make them life Che, Vilma and Fidel anymore." But here in the land of Gregorio Luperón y Tina Bazuca, the Ches, Vilmas and Fidels walk the streets, confidently and serenely, focused on their mission.

Propaganda

If you listen to the seven p.m. or eleven p.m. mainstream news on Telesistema 11 and Tele Canal 16, or if you read the headlines of *El Listen Diario* or *Diario Libre,* you would never know there is an ongoing war of repression against popular resistance. Where do the names of Furi and Quibio Estrella belong in the annals of Dominican patriots who have stood up against the dictatorship of the propertied class?

The leadership of *El MPD* and *El FALPO* are referred to as terrorists and armed bandits. This led the majority of people to think they were professional criminals who carried out terrorism against local people for their own gain. The ruling class will never project an image that seeks to elevate the self-image of the oppressed. It is only when the elites —the minority— have the workers —the majority demoralized and dispirited that they can contain them. Every billboard, commercial, news report, curriculum lesson and everything else in class society is dedicated to ensuring that the sleeping giant remains dormant. The MPD never shrunk before this task of finding a way out of the morass.

One day after lunch, I was invited to do a radio interview on U.S. foreign policy. The hosts of the radio program inquired about the U.S.'s building of seven new military bases in Colombia. I launched into an invective against the misnamed "war on drugs" which domestically is nothing more than a war on Black people and poor people; and beyond America's borders, merely a post-Cold War excuse for re-invasion, re-occupation and re-colonization. The radio anchors and producers of the show laughed at the idea of a "gringo revolutionary/MPDista" critical of US foreign policy. One commentator said I should be thankful to my government because, after all, I was free to travel and say whatever I wanted. After sarcastically thanking him for repeating clichés, I explained that first and foremost, I was an internationalist and that I stood for all working people regardless of their language or national origin. I went on to say:

"The US government is not my government and does not act in consultation with the American people. Any opportunities Americans did have were the result of the very negation of those opportunities elsewhere. If my own family members knew what the U.S. was truly responsible for, they too would see things differently. Tragic that many of their minds and hearts are not open enough to take that step."

The MPD tribunes were brilliant orators and interlocutors. Public speaking and writing was part of their training. They were prepared to appear on any panel at a moment's notice. They read every newspaper, domestic and international, and make connections between every unique struggle. I received training from legends and legends in the making.

If only the well-spoken representatives of the silenced could articulate their cause on every news broadcast to fill the airwaves with truth instead of the propagandistic, misogynist venom contained within *telenovelas* (soap operas), talk shows and Don Francisco.

When exiting the radio station, some movement lawyers and professors arranged for me to stay with them for a few days outside of the city to make sure no heat came down on me because of the interview. They joked, but with an undercurrent of seriousness, that soon enough I would be like them, no longer welcome in the country.

A few months later, I was on a bus in San Pedro de Macoris returning to the capital after teaching. It was 8:30 p.m. on a warm Wednesday night. The sun had set and the stars flourished in the sky. The voice on the radio excitedly repeated that armed criminals had attacked and taken over the central police headquarters of Nagua, a town in the north. Anticipating the barrage of bullets the police were about to unleash on them, the FALPO ambushed the precinct, disarming the police and sending them scattering in every direction. Many police could not even muster up the time to strap on and tie their boots. Accustomed to being on the aggressive side of the trigger, they scampered, barefoot, out of the precinct with hot bullets on their heels.

This was the nation's top news story and the National Guard was sent in. I thought about the valiant, selfless warriors on the other side of the country and the war they were engaged in. The defenders of the dispossessed and the soldiers of the future endured relentless assassination plots and massacres that were never mentioned in the media. The usurpers of Dominican self-determination took concrete truth and turned it on its head, making a mockery of objectivity. The mission of seizing the means of communication was not pie in the sky; it was a necessary step in the definitive liberation of humanity.

To Be Somebody

Whatever you needed, Franklin had it. Guns, a safe house, a bodyguard, money, contacts within the police to tip off the movement, counterintelligence, hitmen, lawyers to defend political prisoners, or CO's to smuggle letters and books to comrades in prison. His smile was the key to every vault in Villa Altagracia. He was well-respected and well-loved.

Franklin had a magnetic personality and whenever he entered a room, he left an indelible impression. First of all, he was enormous. He *skyed*[50] over his comrades and heaved rocks further than anybody. It was rumored that he took out his first police officer at a *huelga* (strike) when he was barely twelve years old. When the neighborhood mobilized, the combat-tested youth darted into the streets with bandanas covering their faces and towels soaked in

---

[50] *Skyed* is slang for stood taller than everyone else.

water to withstand the tear gas. But not Franklin. There was no hiding a *dirigente* who stood 6 6', 245 lbs. Everyone knew his stance. When news crews interviewed the balaclava-clad youth, Franklin came out on national television; showing his face, screaming into the cameras and denouncing the politicians and their cronies, unhesitatingly, without fear of the reprisals that would follow, he stated "If the *chivatos* (snitches) and police want to come for me, let them come for me. I won't live in fear in my own country." Due to his presence and the way he took up space, his running mates baptized him *la yegua*, the mare.

La yegua was also a social butterfly. He could talk to the most dispirited grandmother, the loneliest house wife or a classroom full of agitated high school students. He never met an audience he disliked. When he took stage, the room stopped. Audiences were glued to his every word. His mentors bragged that "he threw pages to the left," meaning that he read voraciously to better understand Latin America's history of struggle, and the Dominican Republic's place in this continent wide insurrection. It was these skills that propelled him into a leadership position within el MPD. The top cadre reasoned that once they won over Franklin, they had won over half of Villa Altagracia's 175,000 inhabitants.

Spellbound

Yahaira was from Villa Altagracia as well but she had left with her family to live in Providence when she was three years old. Her father was a highly-respected judge who felt iron hot contempt for Franklin and the *tigueres* (riff-raff) who insisted upon interrupting business with protests that shut down the highways and commerce of the entire town.

Though Yahaira still dreamt in Spanish, truthfully she had a greater command of a foreign tongue. She had graduated at the top of her class as an English/Black Studies major at Princeton University. Every summer she returned home to visit her family. She understood little about the national liberation war, the crucible of fire that gave birth to Franklin and his rage. Late night police raids, going underground for months in a neighboring town and wearing police bullets as badges of honor were as foreign to her as bell hooks, James Baldwin, Jesmyn Ward and Richard Wright were to Franklin.

Two destinies, drifting in different life orbits, collided in the summer of 2009. Yahaira was out partying with her cousins when she met Franklin who worked as a bouncer at Villa Altagracia's largest club, El Caribe. The first time their eyes interlocked, they both felt their knees wobble.

Yahaira was petite, with, what the locals called, a guitar shaped body. Franklin –in addition to being a colossus- had a face cut of white granite, with sharp angular cheekbones. He was a heartthrob, and knowing as much he used this trait to call upon his female contacts to help the movement out with favors, lending money to the movement or hiding contacts, who were on the run from the state.

The pair attracted a great deal of attention on their own but together they were the talk of the town. Franklin towered over Yahaira and jokingly swept her off her feet and tossed her over his shoulder to tease her. Yahaira searched for a sidewalk or a park bench in order to reach his lips and kiss him. After dating for the summer weeks, they felt such intense passion that they discussed the option of marriage. They decided to tie the knot so that Franklin could eventually be with her in the U.S. The months the newlyweds spent apart from one another marched at a tortoise's pace. Yahaira returned every other month, anticipating the granting of her husband's visa. She became pregnant and now the couple prepared for parenthood with 1,600 miles of distance between them.

After a sixteen month wait, the couple was called to the US embassy. When the consulate agent returned Franklin's passport with a visa, they looked at each other, wondering if they should cry out of celebration or out of fear. For they were about to embark upon a reality that had snuck up on them both, the reality of marriage, twenty four hours a day, seven days a week.

Disillusioned

The marriage was doomed to fail before the pair shared their one thousandth kiss. Franklin had his culture. Yahaira had hers. Franklin was never meant to leave the only surroundings he ever knew. New England would pose a threat to his identity and his ego, more formidable than a politician's bribe or a policeman's bullet.

She lived in Providence with her parents and their newborn baby boy, Johan. Franklin weighed his options. Follow the American dream or remain where he was indispensable. Overnight, Villa Altagracia's highly-decorated marksman became Providence's stay at home dad. When he exited JFK airport without a coat into the Northeast's 23 degree, February weather, he instantly knew he had made a grave mistake. It took less than one week for him to grow depressed with his new reality.

Franklin began to drink and put on weight. Something about American food made him feel lifeless and bloated. He wasn't sharp like he had been and his face grew scruffy. *La yegua* forgot the days before when he rolled out of bed with a glock in one hand and a book in the other. Villa Altagracia's *dirigente* contemplated turning his back on the dream and the dreamers but his pride weighed heavy on the see-saw of identity. How would it look if he returned home – from the country of miracles- empty-handed, plump, soft and defeated?

Dispirited

He who had commanded a people's battalion before the onslaught of military police now changed diapers and heated bottles for a living. Without a dollar to his name, he depended on Yahaira for everything. If he wanted *mofongo*,[51] he had to tell his wife in advance. When they argued about the littlest thing, he raised his voice blaming her for pressuring him into leaving his natural habitat. But his voice dissipated out before her screaming retorts. He tried to

---

[51] A mashed plantain with garlic dish

work but he didn't speak a word of English. Yahaira resented his "ignorance" and wanted her own free time to hang out with the cultivated and educated spoken word crowd that she was accustomed to. The blame game made them both bitter and at twenty three they carried a mutual resentment, usually reserved for a couple twice their age.

Yahaira kicked him out. The man who had 100,000 homes in his old town, had nowhere to go. He roamed the desolate, frost-bitten streets of Providence trying to remember who he was. The first night he slept inside of a Peter Pan bus station. He began to work odd jobs overnight at clubs cleaning up after the last inebriated clientele left at three a.m. He slept on buses during the day. Because of his mare-like size, he was soon asked to work security at the clubs, which was a big upgrade from being an errand boy.

Fortunately for him, Franklin grew up in Villa Altagracia with two second cousins who had immigrated to Providence five years before him. Lost in dead-end, minimum wage jobs that required them to work the graveyard shift, his contemporaries found themselves knee deep in the world of hustling. They sold drugs on La Broa –the main drag in Providence's Dominican community- and in the poor, white suburbs. They told him if he did a 10 pm to 8 a.m. shift with them a few times a week, he could earn $125 cash per night. This new rhythm, combined with $75 all-night shifts as a bouncer, earned him a steady income. He learned to hide crack cocaine under trash cans and waited for junkies to come around who needed it. He led them to it, careful not to pick it up and implicate himself in the distribution process. Other times he brought cocaine directly to white customers who lived in condominiums in Cranston and Pawtucket. When he made a drop off, he waited around for at least twenty minutes, confident his clientele would need a resupply. A few random customers turning into a dozen plus dependents who called him at all times of the day and night. Soon he needed to trade in his old jalopy for a newer Toyota to keep up with the runs. It was an ugly world –far removed from the ideals he came from- but he felt defeated when he considered the options.

Seduced

When you are poor, money is seductive. When your pockets are full, you feel no pain, or so Franklin thought. He did anything to stack up more money. Just as the sun drifts far away from the Northeast in December, leaving New England in a four month frozen stupor, Franklin gravitated away from his former world of conviction and righteous action.

The streets were disorienting and depoliticizing. Quick money brought quick power. Scorned, he refused to check in with Yahaira, passive-aggressively leaving her to think he was dead. When he yearned for her, he focused on the final image he had of her patronizingly cursing him out and slamming the door in his face. For a man whose reputation back home was based on loyalty, this was unforgivable. He would freeze to death before he would crawl back to implore her to let him stay with her and their son Johan, who he affectionately called Bombi. Lost, estranged and muddle-headed, he was at least his own man again. He promised himself, he would never again be anybody's burden.

Unstoppable

Franklin began to lift weights again. He returned to the old form that had earned him his nickname. The local Latino dance clubs hired him as their doorman. No one, regardless of who knew who, could get into the club without settling accounts with him. Sneakers, Timberlands, baggy jeans, hoodies, and "a sausage fest" were all justifications for a de facto fine, imposed by Providence's smooth-talking, Dominican doorman. If he suspected the revelers carried marijuana, ecstasy or mollies, he patted them down and seized their drugs. He pretended to throw them away in disgust, only to hold on to them and resell the narcotics back to the post three a.m. crowd at inflated rates. Now he flipped thousands of dollars in a weekend. He arrived at daybreak to his cousins' apartment, squinting as the blinding sun rose above him, smuggling its rays through the curtain blinds. Exhausted but accomplished, he threw down hundreds of crumpled bills onto his mattress. He didn't even count the money as he neatly folded it into stacks, but he knew that thousands of dollars were flowering into tens and hundreds of thousands of dollars. He despised money but grew addicted to the freedom it signified. Having never opened a bank account nor written a check, he opted for a safe in the back of his trunk. Underneath his work out gear, protein shakes and supply of daily fruit, he hid stacks of money in a small safe where most car-owners have a spare tire.

Estranged

He had not seen his son, Bombi in six months. More hard-headed than ever, he vowed to see Bombi but without exchanging a single word with Yahaira.

Both mother and son were elated to see the gentle giant. He held his prodigy for ten minutes and silently listened to her half-apologetic, self-righteous diatribe before condescendingly tossing a tightly taped, thrice folded trash bag at her. Before she could count the four thousand plus dollars in cash distributed in four envelopes, Franklin had descended back to the street. She called after him, but all he heard were the texts coming into his phone from three other girls.

Coveted

Money is freedom and he who has it is the freest of free men; he who doesn't is a prisoner to scarcity. Franklin was propelled to local stardom. Fast cash meant nicer clothes, a new SUV, street credibility and an abundance of women to blow his money on.

Franklin was inside of one woman, thinking about three others. Before returning to one girlfriend, he saved numerous text messages to drafts in his phone so that he could later send them quick and not provoke her jealousy. He carried two phones, one for profits and one for expenses. No girl he dated knew this so he could never be caught red handed. He couldn't be in the here and now because he was always everywhere, anticipating the next adventure. Hustling was his addiction and dating multiple women was merely an extension of the constant adventure.

He, who was once somebody, then nobody, emerged as somebody again. He took all of his people skills, and without a revolutionary outlet, invested them in the world of hustling. He had two cars. An old beat up 1995 Geo Tracker jeep, for drop-offs and collections, and a $50,000 silver 2009 Escalade, to show off on the town. Every time the police stopped him in his larger-than-life Cadillac, he wore a smirk on his face, as they unsuccessfully searched for illegal narcotics. Although he felt a deep-seated anger towards the ghetto surveillance, he was polite as a UN diplomat, addressing them with his thick accent, but maintaining a formal demeanor, just to rub it in their faces that he was one step ahead of them.

One Saturday night, a young drunk driver rear-ended his car. Panic stricken, Franklin gave the petrified, inebriated teenager $800 and told him to get lost. His destiny was precarious and tragedy was only one 911 call away.

Loyal

Franklin rented a permanent hotel room in Washington Heights, Providence and Brockton. Other drug dealers paid him to crash there so he, again, came out winning.

Out of touch with his MPD family, *la yegua* stopped reading and projecting their unique worldview. Still, he was not your average hustler. He applied his acumen for revolutionary action to street adventurism. With all of the women he chased, he picked up Portuguese and Cape Verdean Kreolu. He became fluent and was soon a polyglot. Franklin, who only six months before was a sloth, still in pajamas and in a bathrobe at one in the afternoon, couching it up with a three-year-old, was now on the move. And nothing could stop him.

Still, he was careful not to squander money. He was generous but intelligent. But when it came to women, he knew how to throw down. On a double date his *pana* (partner) scrutinized the check in front of two Brazilian girls. Franklin rapidly but calmly grabbed the bill out of his hand, without the girls noticing. He switched the conversation, hiding the check under the table. Without confirming the exact price, he removed four $100 bills from his pocket and placed them with the check in the waitress's folder. Later that night he told his *pana full*[52], "Never review a check in front of women. Cover it and figure it out later but never flinch in front of a woman."

Invincible

La yegua cornered markets in Providence, Boston, the Bronx and everywhere in between. He checked in with his *compañeros* back home in Villa Altagracia but felt worlds removed from their everyday struggles.

This was the era when Dominican baseball players were beginning to dominate Major League Baseball. Manny Ramirez, David Ortiz and Pedro Martinez were rewriting baseball as America knew it. Franklin wore a Red Sox hat everywhere he went. Some Yankee fans challenged his right to represent the Red Sox South of Bridgeport, Connecticut. These incidents were never uptown or in the Bronx, where everyone knew him and the masses of Dominicans were also rooting for the Red Sox. Twice Yankee fans –South of 96th St.- made fun of his jersey and spit on him during the 2005 Red Sox-Yankee playoff series. He calmly left them both in a pool of blood and exited the scene before they could make heads or tails of the situation. It was not his style to look for problems but he resolved them when he had to.

Yahaira reached out to her old confidante to patch things ups. Villa Altagracia's most humble was seeing so much money he told her, her uppity judge father and her Princeton education, to go fuck

---

[52] Spanglish slang for a close partner.

themselves. He still visited his son once every few weeks but the visits were brief. When there were dollar signs to be stacked, little else mattered. Now Yahaira was the one who talked to a voicemail.

Alienated

He hated who he had become but he no longer knew who he was. He was illegal. He never followed up with his immigration appointments. He wasn't a slave to anyone's caprices, not Yahaira's, her well-off parents nor those of Rhode Island's courts.

He still had his political training but the ego is a terrible thing. It spiraled out of control. He endeared himself with women using his *muela* (game) and soft smile to charm them. He never slept in the same place. That was a decision he made after midnight. If a woman was well-off and acted drunk and sloppy, he pocketed what he could from her purse or apartment. The street reasoning was that if anyone "got caught slipping,"[53] they themselves were to blame. Besides, he concluded, the money he expropriated funded the movement back home. His moral code grew out of the stark social contrasts that characterized his Dominican homeland. He was lost but loyal, a hustler, but a hustler who hammered out a revolutionary street ethics, and refused to take advantage of his own people.

The chase became an addiction. But no one can live on a permanent high. With the women he enamored, he mentioned using a condom but in the heat of the passion it was a hindrance and he rarely used one. He had more than one scare with pregnancies and STD's. The ebbs and flows began to play with his mind. He wondered how many "hustlers" would today be a Bunchie Carter or Fred Hampton[54] if there was a community to invest in them, applying their "conversation" and talents to the future.

---

[53] Made a mistake and acted careless
[54] Two slain leaders of the Black Panther Party.

Reunited

The Secretariat, the highest body of the MPD, flew an elder leader, Felix, a veteran of the 1965 revolution, to Providence to reel Franklin back in. Felix trained Franklin, his godson, in Marxist ideology and street tactics ten years before. The leadership was deeply saddened, first by Franklin's abrupt self-exile and then, by his fall from revolutionary grace.

They sat down to dinner. Felix threw his hands up in disbelief: "Who have you become? This is what we taught you? You are that weak that for some rum, yankee dollar signs and women, you are going to sell us out?" He was both angry and ashamed. He fired back: "Fuck the movement! This is a different world. What is the movement doing for me?" He knew he was wrong to betray three generations of self-sacrificing MPD warriors, but a broken heart and bruised ego conspired against his MPD training. A satellite out of orbit, his feet could not find any familiar ground to touch.

Felix and his godson never even started their meal. Franklin jumped up pushing his seat back, asserting "I don't know who I am anymore." He sent the sixty three year old warrior off with a hurried apology, a trash bag full of Jordan sneakers, new designer clothes and a tightly wrapped plastic bag. Disgusted, Felix threw the bag into his suitcase in the trunk of his brother-in-law's car. Three weeks later he delivered the trash bag to three MPD leaders in Villa Altagracia's humble El Caobal neighborhood. The tightly wrapped double trash bag had $7,000 in it, and a note that read "We all have a role to play. Keep playing yours and I will play mine."

Resurrected

Just as fast as his star had rose in the north, Franklin again fell from glory. His own cousins, jealous of his ascendance, which left them no room to operate, tipped off the police that the trunk of his Geo Tracker was lined with cocaine. Franklin again returned to *nobodydom*.

The state sent the popular agitator to languish in a cell, where he nostalgically remembered what it felt like to be somebody. A federal judge from Arizona determined that he would be deported, but not before he served twelve years in a federal prison. After two months in the same federal penitentiary where Leonard Peltier[55] was held, Leavenworth, Kansas, he received a package from Santo Domingo. He unwrapped the package and took out three books, Eduardo Galeano's The Open Veins of Latin America, The Communist Manifesto, and Pedro Mir's[56] Hay un Pais en el Mundo. He took a deep breath, kissed a picture of his son, Bombi and opened The Communist Manifesto. There was an inscription from Felix: "We all have a role to play." He began to read, realizing he was just beginning to live.

"I Can't Be Bought"

Pololo oversaw the leadership in La Linea, the Northwest corridor of the Dominican Republic. He prepared notoriously massive feasts that knocked out his guests, who then needed two hour naps in a hammock to recuperate their strength. One day, in 2008, as he sat down to eat with his guests, two younger student comrades, there was a knock at the door. He scurried toward his bedroom, opened the door and ushered his visitors in. He handed them a tape recorder and ordered them, "Stay right here in my bedroom. You'll be able to overhear this. Catch this! Catch this!"

Anxiously exited the room, Pololo greeted a well-dressed official at the front door. A master of small talk and a cunning conversationalist, Pololo killed time, eliciting as much information from the official as he could. After a half hour, the undercover DNI official said his piece.[57] He leaned over with a blank check and told the young revolutionary, "You fill that in." He offered him a scholarship to Madrid or Barcelona. He ended by saying "My doors

---

[55] Leonard Peltier is a leader of the American Indian Movement and is one of the longest held political prisoners in America.

[56] Dominican national poet.

[57] The DNI is the National Department of Investigations, the Dominican CIA.

are always open to you. You draft the proposal and I'll sign off on it. We want to work with you Pololo, not against you."

Why didn't the newspapers write on this story? The campaign of disinformation against El FALPO divided the public and turned many an honest citizen against them, the forces best positioned to defend their collective class interests. The media functioned as the fifth branch of government. Where are the articles that seek to humanize the media's *tigueres* (thugs/criminals) and counteract all of the dishonest state propaganda?

Pololo had power. Other leaders had been bought off. The ruling class feared the FALPO's leadership so much that they were willing to employ him and bribe him in hopes of taking him out of action. Pololo responded with his usual frivolity. If you did not know him well, you would have thought his warm smile and cordiality signified that he accepted the deal. He walked the intelligence officer out, addressing him as Señor Lopez and politely declined the offer. He promised that the two would meet soon enough but in a different arena of struggle. His confidence struck fear into the intelligence officer. Like two generals on opposing sides of the battlefield, they showed one another mutual respect. Now, there were no goodbyes, only silence.

Plucked from the Streets

The revolutionary code is to never forget the fallen or the incarcerated. Taking care of the *dirigentes* on the inside, in prison, is a must. Adonai —a leading militant of Moca— had been in prison for the past six years because he was accused of killing a snitch and an undercover cop. His father Don Cheo (Mr. Cheo) told me that we had to be up at 4 a.m. on a Sunday to catch the first bus, in order to get in line to get into the prison. His brother, Cata —short for *catastrophe*— figured we should not even bother sleeping, since we had to catch the bus so early. He wanted to break night partying.[58] I didn't realize at the time what I was getting into. Cata had a bad

---

[58] New York City slang for stay up all night.

cocaine problem. Every ten minutes he mumbled unintelligible things about El FALPO and how we'll "fuck everyone up tonight and shoot them if we have to."

It was now 2 a.m. and there was nowhere else to sleep. I was trapped. Cata proposed that we buy drinks for two female hustlers and then kick them money to sleep with us. I remember thinking five times that night that Adonai's brother, Cata was going to get me killed. I argued with him and tried to yell over him and the loud music: "*Maldito loco* (You damned crazy man) I have to be at your father's house and we have to be up in a few hours to get your nephew and go to the jail, La Victoria."[59]

Luckily, we stumbled upon some other FALPO leaders who were out and about. I gave them a look that spoke to how different these two brothers —Adonai and Cata— could be. Their smirks signified that I should have known what I was getting myself into. They intervened and brought Cata and I to his father's house. We skirted through some dirt alleys and Cata yelled for his father to open the door to the one-room wooden hovel. His father, Don Cheo, woke up screaming at him "Why are you always waking me up in the middle of the night? You idiot!" Arriving at the door with nothing on but underwear and flip-flops, he smacked Cata on the head with an infamous *cocotazo*.[60] He greeted me half-asleep and told me to lie down on his bed for a few hours before we caught the first bus into the Capital. He laid down beside me on the small bed and I fell into a deep slumber.

Two hours later, Don Cheo woke me up. I was absolutely exhausted. In my twenties, I had the energy to experience these all-night, revolutionary bouts. But that was ten years prior. My head was spinning from the exhaustion. He gave me some soap and sent me to the outhouse where the latrine and shower were. It was pitch-dark and I had no toilet paper. I swung the rickety door open and I plopped down on the wooden toilet seat. In one fell swoop, I plummeted to the ground. As I fell, I grabbed the door to brace myself. My feet swung up over my head. The makeshift latrine seat

---

[59]Damn crazy man.
[60] Slap on top of the head

had collapsed under my weight and now the doorway was falling on top of me. The small bathroom hovel had caved in. I laughed so hard in disbelief that I couldn't stand up. Fortunately the latrine hole was far too small for me to fall through. Don Cheo heard the commotion and ran back out with his candle. He apologized out of embarrassment. I apologized for having wrecked his john. We shrugged off the mishap and continued on with our mission: to bring Adonai some books, *yucca con pollo*,[61] and *cariño* (affection).

The rest of Adonai's family met us in front of the jail to make the queue together. Adonai's winsome five-year-old son, Carlito was restless in the long queue and was jumping on top of me. He wanted to play. He was going to see his father in La Victoria prison for the fourth time in the past three weeks and fifth time in his life. He lived in Boston with his mom, who was also an MPD militant.

When we finally passed through the burdensome security and strip searches, Adonai hugged me and held onto me. Every few minutes he pressed his forehead into my cheek and clasped onto me, thanking me for coming to visit him. He was starved for decent critical literature, movement and affection. I asked him if he had been able to form revolutionary cells on the inside. He responded that there were a few like-minded inmates but the preponderance of petty hustlers and snitches made it tough. He sent me back to Moca with a laundry list of tasks to carry out. Though his body was encaged, his heart and imagination still walked the streets of his old stomping grounds.

I reminded him of the night we danced *palos* in Villa Altagracia. *Palos* is an Afro-Dominican dance ceremony that a community dances to the beat of drums. That night, overcome by a trance, their bodies became zombified and they moved and danced as though possessed. Gyrating uncontrollably, they fell to the earth and violently shook over the rocks, dirt and concrete. Other FALPistas held Adonai, to make sure he did not smash his head into the ground. The next day they fervently denied that a spirit had entered their beings. What happens at the fiesta de palos stays at the

---

[61] Cassava with chicken.

fiesta de palos. *Mamajuana,* or Dominican style moonshine, drums and the ancestors were a powerful combination.

Convicted of terrorizing the neighborhood terrorizers, Adonai vowed to carry on his commitment regardless of the challenges. We sat in a circle and reminisced about how freely Adonai had run the streets as the wrath of the poor. He asked about all of his MPD family on the outside and vowed to carry on the struggle for El Barrio Furi (named after one of our previous heroes), no matter where they imprisoned him physically. He swore revenge on an assortment of unpopular local petty oppressors. When the authorities threatened to relocate him to a prison in the east of the island, his hometown erupted, swearing infinite chaos if he was transported further away from them. He has defended them and they defended him until the end.

When it was time to leave, Carlito hung on to his father, refusing to let go. He wanted to know why he couldn't exit with the rest of us and walk out freely. With tears welling up in our eyes, we calmly explained this was a university where his papá studied. Outside, I reassured Carlito he had the best dad in the world and before long his courses at the University of Freedom would be over and he would be home with his family.

There is too much Trauma

Jose Rafael Garcia —alias Bili— was and continues to be an evil, sick, broken man. He was a military officer who used his power to rape and kill. He trapped women inside a hospital where he was a night watchman and took advantage of them. There was a deep hatred of life posited in his scrawny, chestnut face. Bili destroyed the lives of women who only wanted to raise their children and give selflessly of themselves to their families.

A local committee of the FALPO gathered together to plot popular vengeance against Billy. The police could not be counted upon to carry out redemption. However, when the people's vigilantes made their move, Billy was ready. The corrupt lieutenant gunned down two brave leaders, including a student leader named Luis. El FALPO tallied up the rape charges and the deaths he caused. He had five strikes against him. Usually one strike sealed your fate. When the citizenry was mistreated, they did not call the police; they called the FALPO to defend them. Equipped with the hitmen of the mafia and the sensitivity of a team of social workers, the FALPO earned a reputation as professional "fixers." Ray Donovan was hollywood; the FALPO was real life.

Bili was hated by the community. What social forces called such a beast into being? The price on his head was high. He realized he could not outrun El FALPO. He turned himself in and voluntarily went to jail. He reasoned that this was his only chance to live. On the other side of the concrete bars, Billy became a "reformed" Evangelical preacher. With nowhere else to flee, he hid behind God. He sent word to those hunting him down that he had re-found himself and renounced his sins. He went to the very jail where FALPistas were incarcerated because they had dared to avenge his crimes but were outgunned.

Though Bili professed to be a changed man, the enemies he had made did not buying his timely conversion. Back on the outside El FALPO distributed flyers to his congregation of over thirty people citing his crimes against women and families. They spray-painted "Rapist" and "Murderer" on his place of worship. Can rapists and murderers change overnight by precipitously embracing God? Was his life safe or did it still hang in the balance?

One night we walked through the martyr Luis' old neighborhood, which he had presided over with respect and humility. My nieces informed me that the teenage girl on a porch adjacent to us was Luis' daughter. She was listening to Sensato's Dominican remix of Rick Ross' "You Don't Even Know It."[62] The seductive beat blared out over the entire neighborhood. She was only thirteen years old but could have passed for sixteen or seventeen. I commented on how mature she looked for her age. My nieces chimed in with local folklore saying that this was because she was raped and when a girl was raped she quickly developed into a

---

[62] https://www.youtube.com/watch?v=YTIWS2yX8yc

woman.   I reflected on the local scuttlebutt and moved the conversation forward. I did the math. She was in her mom's belly when Luis was mowed down by the assassin Billy. My nieces, who have known her since she was little, told me she was curious about her father and who he was. I approached and asked her if she had any pictures of her dad. I asked her if she wanted to hear more about her father's character and commitment to others.   I learned to tread light around the dead, not remembering or invoking the deceased, lest the nostalgia stir fresh feelings of tragedy among the family. I read the spirit of the room and followed accordingly. She was eager to hear more about her dad. I showed her pictures and painted a portrait of the principled, balanced, rank and file soldier that her father was.

Twelve years had passed since Luis' unnatural death. In the heart of Luis' comrades, the desire to off Billy was stronger than ever. Billy walks, prays and preaches in the shadow of death.

To Live like Amín

FELABEL stood for El Frente Estudiantil Amín Abel (Student Front Amín Abel), named after the Dominican revolutionary, Amín Abel Hasbun.   The FALPO responded to the grievances that emerged from the *barrios* (neighborhoods) and the FELABEL coordinated a student movement to fight rising tuition costs. To understand the mission of the FELABEL, it is necessary to grasp the vision of the martyr who inspired its foundation.

Amín Abel Hasbun was an engineer of Palestinian roots who became an MPD leader in the 1960's. Outraged at the lack of educational opportunities for working class students, Amín led a hunger strike at la Universidad Autónoma de Santo Domingo (U.A.S.D.), demanding access to higher education for the country's poor. He went on to participate in the popular battalions that fought the 1965 U.S. occupation, before he joined the underground of the MPD. Known for his keen dominion of historical materialism and his massive sense of humility, Amín helped train the first generation of MPD dirigentes.   On September 24th, 1970, Dominican intelligence agents raided his home and killed him in cold blood, in front of his pregnant wife and one-year-old child. Amín was 28.

El FELABEL: The Student Movement

La U.A.S.D. (pronounced La Was) is a sprawling campus, with dozens of entrances, home to over 200,000 working-class Dominican students. It was a hotbed of revolutionary ferment and clashes with the police. Every time the government threatened to raise tuition, the FELABEL and other student organizations mobilized the student body. Hundreds of students traded their button-down shirts for t-shirts, their polished shoes for sneakers, tied a bandana around their faces and headed to the exit gates to shut down the city's traffic. After the police had entered the campus and shot three students dead in 1999, popular pressure forced the government to pass a law that the military could not enter or fire into university grounds. Once the students went beyond the universities' gates, it remained to be seen who would have more injured and martyred, the police or the students.

Los hijos de papimami (the sons and daughters of the rich) studied at UTESA, PUCAMAIMA or one of the other private universities. They made fun of the U.A.S.D., portraying it as a cross between a circus and a ghetto. The running joke was that it took U.A.S.D. students ten years to obtain an undergraduate degree because there were so many protests on campus that students could not complete the semester and receive their credits. There was a certain truth to this claim but el FELABEL did not organize student strikes willy-nilly, as their detractors claimed.

What the *tutumpotes*[63] (slang for the rich) failed to understand, through their prism of privilege, was that the low tuition was a lifeline for poor students. Any increase in the cost of public transportation or admission affected tens of thousands of students.

In reference to the privileged layers of students, who sought to discredit the FELABEL's work, one leader, Química stated: "The *tutumpotes* can travel abroad and study wherever they want. We don't have that luxury. This is not New York City, where city authorities can arbitrarily raise the cost of the subway and tolls and motorists and commuters —acting like hot airbags—do little besides complain. This is Santo Domingo —where we seize the time and take our destiny back into our own hands."

Dominican governance had to carefully calculate the repercussions for leveling fresh taxes on the student body. If the ruling cirlces pushed too hard, they understood they could have a revolutionary situation on their hands.

---

[63] Derived from the English word, totem pole.

El FELABEL

Rescuing Memory

La U.A.S.D. was a bastion of the anti-imperialist movement. The campus was a world unto itself, seemingly far removed from the stark inequalities outside of its gates. Virtually free, the U.A.S.D. was a social leveler, in the sense that any poor family could send their children there. There were eight leftist student groups that worked together to mobilize the 200,000 plus student body. Study groups focused on the Soviet experience, the leadership of the Chinese revolution, The Origin of the Family, Private Property and the State, Haitian and Dominican history and Reconstruction and the Civil War in the United States. In the words of Amín, "nothing human is foreign to me." The FELABEL leadership understood this quote to mean that they should be capable of feeling any suffering around the world, as if the pain were their own.

To walk the pathways that cut through the different academic buildings, was to walk on hallowed ground. The campus served as a communist museum, a tribute to decades of international resistance. Perched high above the Department of Science was a life-size painting of Chris Hani, Stephen Biko and the South African, Namibian and Angolan liberation movements. Behind the Sociology Department, there were images of Bobby Sands and the Irish Republican Army, alongside Leila Khaled and the Palestinian Liberation Organization. The visitor remained awestruck, suspended in time and memory. On la U.A.S.D. campus, the Sandinistas mingled with Gaddafi, the Red Guard and the Basque independence movement. The murals of John Brown, Ida B. Wells, General Harriet Tubman and Malcolm X were proof of the internationalist spirit of the campus. The mosaic of murals transported the visitor to la U.A.S.D. to a serene, distant land, free of need and neglect.

Conflagrations

It was a Saturday when the dean and a new board of directors —in an attempt to push the university's direction to the right— instructed the police to destroy and paint over the collection of murals. In flagrant violation of university sovereignty, the police lined up marksman to "protect" the officers assigned to paint over the murals.

Student contacts immediately alerted the president of FELABEL, Elizabeth. Elizabeth alerted Sandra, Caridad and Graciela, who were on campus, leading a study group on capitalism, sexism and women's liberation. A contingent of FELABEL women leaders rushed to confront the desecration of popular memory. The haughty line of police laughed at the dozen women who raced toward them. An avalanche of stones wiped the smirks off of their faces, as they scrambled for cover.

When a senior officer pistol-whipped the highly respected Elizabeth, all hell broke loose. The dirigentes made a series of phone calls. Reinforcements arrived and the crowd continued to swell until it overwhelmed the police lines. Now 200 ideological offspring of Amín Abel surrounded the police, chanting taunts at them and threatening them if they did not leave. A fire wall of women leaders protected the murals.

Outnumbered and overwhelmed, the police speed-walked toward the gates that led to the outside world. The paid enforcement knew this was their enemies' base. They wanted to flee before the balance of forces shifted more in their disfavor.

Elizabeth's nose was shattered, yet she continued to respond to the situation. A field general, she took care of herself later; first she had to take care of her FELABEL *compañeros*. While pinching her nose to stop the river of blood, she gave an interview to a news channel on the wanton police violations. Confident and even-tempered, Elizabeth never hurled any personal insults at the police but rather focused her ire on the political establishment that sought to divorce the student body from its political heritage. A line of women formed around her, in case the police tried to take advantage of the fact that the student leaders were on the parameter of the university.

Student organizations pitched tents and camped outside, until they were sure their campus was safe. The police did not dare enter again. Other FELABEL women's committees across the country sent reinforcements and supplies. If the police decided to attack, they would be taking on a superior army. Taking shifts sleeping, they gathered around a bonfire, sharing poetry, anecdotes and visions. They stood united, as Amín and his co-conspirators had a generation before. The hunger-striking, engineering student gave birth to their valiant lineage and now they would preserve it for future generations. La U.A.S.D was teeming with resistance; the resistance naturally selected the next generation of Amín Abels.

Combatting Sexual Violence

The women's front was an important part of the MPD's work. Building upon the selfless example of Mamá Tingó, La Coronela Gladys Borrel, Piky Lora, Tiny Bazooka, the Mirabal Sisters and so many other anonymous Dominican women, the women FALPistas elevated the image of Dominican women.

Gender imbalances and a predominance of male leadership were a concrete problem in the left movement. This was not a footnote to the MPD's story but rather a major problem that had to be overcome. Machismo was an undeniable fact in both the D.R. and in the United States. There were women protagonists but there were also meetings where there were twenty men and one or two women.

The legacy of sexism was strong and manifested itself in both mundane and extraordinary ways. The crime statistics for the first six months of this year in the Capital, Santo Domingo are telling. According to the police there were 10,585 reports of major domestic violence against women in those six months. This tally did not include all of the women who were intimidated into silence and did not report the abuse. To put this number in perspective, at the same time there were less drug related incidents, 8,726 that were reported to the police.[64] The FALPO took aim at local perpetrators of

---

[64] Sension Villalona.

misogyny and conducted popular education to empower women through organizing.

Mario Jose was a local *marpiolo* or pimp. He owned a brothel under a bridge at the entrance of one of Bani's poorest neighborhoods, Villa Bisonó. He abused women and was known as an arrogant, gun-wielding intimidator. Gathering together a clandestine nucleus of cadre, the FALPO showed up unannounced at the cabaret looking for Mario Jose but the sly, unscrupulous businessman had escaped. A warning was extended to the women sex workers forced into this harrowing reality. Within minutes the bar, dance floor and stretch of makeshift rooms was set ablaze and burnt to a crisp. Local women leaders expressed that the ashes were a memorial to the essence of capitalism—greed, misogyny and debauchery.

At the same time, the protagonists of the popular act realized that this center of degradation was the group of women's only source of income. The brothel had been flattened and was smoldering under their feet. What replacement jobs could the FALPO offer the local women? The revolution did not move forward on a smooth, linear path. It claimed thousands of victims for daring to take on the insidiousness that envelops millions.

The incidence of sexual violence, AIDS, brothels and alcoholism was a direct measurement of how oppressed a community was. In some *campos* and *barrios,* sexual abuse was rampant; scarcely a child has escaped.[65] Barrero was one such village. Few places on earth were home to such a high concentration of misery. Some of the symptoms of underdevelopment included unemployment, humiliation, alcoholism, illiteracy, sexism, child abuse and the proliferation of 7th Day Adventist churches. The children had almost no chance to come of age unscathed. When "good Christians" warned of the hell that awaited the unfaithful, the MPD leadership inquired about the hell that today encaged the most faithful. No one had to look without to find hell. Home was hell. The sons and daughters who have emerged from the inferno had nothing to lose but their trauma.

---

[65] Rural towns and urban ghettos.

The community called in the MPD, in hopes that an outside intervention could curb the systematic abuse of children. El FALPO gathered fifty children and teenagers into a circle and gave a workshop on exposing and resisting sexual assault and the importance of safe sex for teenagers. After a positive, interactive dialogue and snack, there were dozens of accusations emerging about Roberto, Miguel Angel, Fausto and other known molesters. Children and teenagers —their innocence abducted— told shockingly similar tales about the sexual abuse they endured. Parents and families began to gather around to listen. At last, the children were allowed to speak, without being judged or blamed. With the truth revealed, the parents and community wanted blood.

A lynch mob emerged and descended after one of the accused rapists. Fausto was already on the run. He sensed the vengeance in the air and left the village on a moped. The FALPO dispatched troops to assist the families in writing a report at the police headquarters. The bloodthirsty mob headed back over the hill to where Miguelangel lived. Encircling him, they repeated verbatim the accusations of dozens of little girls. He stuttered and mentioned something about giving them sugar and treats and then *Boom Boom*…two punches later he was unconscious. His neighbors and family members shuffled in and out of their doorways. His blood trickled off of Robertico's hands.

The days passed and Robertico —a FALPO veteran— could still see and feel Miguelangel's blood on his knuckles. Was this healing? Was this justice for the traumatized and the traumatizer? At the time, Robertico was 24, a survivor of sexual abuse himself. He didn't have the broader understanding that he would develop. Bubbled up in him like a volcano, his rage threatened to explode. With time, he reached the conclusion that the victimizers were often victims themselves, who were in need of healing and rehabilitation. Others he reasoned were demented and destroyed, too far gone to play a constructive role in this world. But at that moment, he only had rage and vengeance in his heart. The struggle opened up his heart, where he reserved a place for the perfect love, as well as the perfect hatred.

Libations

The FALPO combined the heroic with the human, the epic with the everyday.

Like the man of steel himself, Leonel got his start in the movement as a professional bank robber.[66] Brazen and emotionless, he oversaw "recuperations." "Recuperations from below" targeted big property owners that had a debt with the people for expropriation. Their money and property were turned over to those who needed it most.

Leonel was fleet of foot, athletic, seemingly untouchable and bulletproof. He had a way of speaking that left outsiders in the dark about what was transpiring. For example, in his coded sentences bullets were *habichuelas* (beans) and the arrival of the police was described as "the cutting of branches." Objective reality forced these warriors to invent a coded slang, unique to their underground struggles. Visitors struggled with the rapid fire cadence of the Guinean and Senegalese-influenced Spanish spoken in the Dominican Republic. Leonel —a practical joker and professional ball-breaker— enjoyed mimicking the accents of comrades from the interior.

Química was a massive, Beowulf-esque *campesino* (peasant) leader, from San Juan de la Maguana, in the south who came to study Chemistry at la U.A.S.D., hence his nickname. Leonel enjoyed pretending to be Química and played the role of a lumbering, uncoordinated giant, mocking the words the country bumpkin struggled to pronounce. Everyone got a big kick out of his antics.

---

[66] This is a reference to Joseph Stalin who continues to be one of the most vilified leaders in history. Before reaching the summits of leadership within the Bolshevik party, Joseph Vissarionovich Djugashvili (known to the world as Stalin) was a tenacious fighter against Russian autocracy. No one can take away his initial contributions to the party of Lenin, Trotsky and the oppressed peoples of Russia. One of his early roles, was that of social bandit; he robbed banks and trains to fund the workers' party.

Leonel convinced Química one night to drink rum with him and a crew of his bandits. The crew was in front of La U.A.S.D. —the first university the Spanish established in their colonies. Hundreds had congregated earlier that day for protests against tuition hikes. Química had never drunk hard liquor before. That night of rum and coca cola was unforgettable. By the time the dawn had emerged, Química had gifted most of my physical possessions to different friends that he had made. Química awoke to a one room studio apartment without his stove top oven, microwave or mattress.

What had gotten into him? Brugal![67] The rum —made of local sugar cane— activated a side of the big lumberjack no one had ever seen. Leonel defended himself, saying "Hey I tried to stop you but there was no stopping the big fella. He wanted everyone to move in with him and share everything him had." Even in a drunken stupor, Química was faithful to his communal ideals.

Fernando had his own issues with drinking. Alcohol was the voice of the voiceless, the expression of the unexpressed. Usually quiet and mild-mannered, the alcohol transformed the tall, wiry Fernando into a viscous and vile character. Just past midnight he turned tables over and defied anyone to step up to him. When he found a rival willing to challenge his prowess, he motioned back at Química, Leonel and the crew to step up on his behalf. Lost in their own revelry —with nothing to prove— they laughed at Fernando's request as if to say *Oh no you got yourself into this tough guy. Good luck.* When Fernando was surrounded by a group of ruffians, the *dirigentes* recognized them from the student movement. They gave them a wink and passed out some plastic cups filled with shots and deescalated the situation. Leonel drove him home and at a later date warned Fernando about further episodes of liquid courage.

Recuperations

Seven years later, Leonel was assigned to recover money from a local pimp and misogynist. This was his umpteenth

---

[67] Popular Dominican rum owned by one of the most elite families in the country.

"robbery" or "recovery" depending on whose side you were on. He set fire to a brothel but was shot six times in the back fleeing the scene. Fortunately, his companions carried him away before he bled to death. His comrades brought the long sought-after Ned Kelly for care on the western side of the island so that no one spotted him.[68]

He who was once invincible and irresistible to the ladies, now needed help with his ileostomy. It was difficult for his comrades-in-arms to visit him. Confined to a wheel chair where he sat wearing a diaper under his dungarees, he still had that wide, confident smile but it surfaced more cautious than before.

The state rewarded those who have sacrificed the most for the people with lead, concrete bars and wooden coffins. Yet, even though they knew the consequences, they persevered forward, serving the people the best way they know how.

Years later, his comrades encountered Leonel's family at a picnic at a local canal. They made the rounds extending their hands to three generations of his family, inquiring about how they were doing. They were careful not to mention what had happened nor conjure up any images that would take the family down nostalgia lane. His father would not shake the hands of the *dirigentes*. Some of Leonel's uncles took their hands but would not make eye contact. Her mother and brother walked with Química and Fernando, explaining the mixed feelings that they had encountered. There was no need for explanations. The FALPO family understood. But who was responsible for his paralysis? The blood was not on the movement's hands but on the forces that obligated people to come into the streets and stand up for their dignity and rights. What was Leonel but a living testament to the violence that systemic violence produced? Now that their greatest defenders were paralyzed and others were buried, the community suffered on in silence, hoping for handouts from the *gringos*, without an eloquent voice to scream

---

[68] Ned Kelly was a famous Irish bandit who waged war on the wealthy of the newly colonized Australia.

forth their name.[69] This was after all what imperialism strived for, peace; the peace that presides over a cemetery.

The *Patria's* Soldiers are Everywhere[70]

The intensity of class struggle in the Dominican Republic is more sustained than in the U.S. Because the level of living is lower in the colonial outposts, the resistance takes on a higher form. There are those whose bodies were forced to migrate but whose hearts stayed behind, loyal to the homeland they loved.

Rhadames and Dagoberto were legends of the 1965 April War. Persecuted by *La Banda Colorá* and marginalized economically, they were forced to move to 137th street and Dyckman Ave. respectively. They resided in Washington Heights, the two poles of the largest Dominican community outside of the nation's capital. Thousands of miles away from home, they continued to do what they knew best— teach the upcoming generations about their Dominican culture and agitate against that *Balaguerismo* that continued to afflict their *patria.*

On July 3rd 1992, the police murdered Jose "Kiko" Garcia on 163rd St, the heart of the Dominican community in Washington Heights. This incident came on the heels of years of police abuse and sent the community into an uproar. The next night one MPDista in exile declared: "Independence Day Yankees! You want fireworks? We'll give you fireworks." A veteran of 1965, he led a squadron of flying guerrillas up Broadway with a squirt gun full of gasoline. He sprayed shots of gasoline under the wheels of the police cars that the crowd came across. Another MPD militant came running by minutes later, tossing lit matches into the small puddles of gasoline, destroying the hated paddy-wagons in a blaze of glory. Sharpshooters mounted the roofs of Washington Heights declaring

---

[69] *Gringos* is a reference to the NGO's. Locals often just say "why don't the gringos come here to help us build our homes," in reference to foreign missionaries and charity workers.

[70] Patria is fatherland.

war on a corrupt, abusive and white supremacist police department. For six days and nights, the streets of Uptown Manhattan were turned into a Licey or Navarrete, the cities in the Dominican Republic with the reputations for the fiercest attacks on the police. And when the infuriated masses ran out of bullets, they made it hail bricks, bottles and rocks on those humid, courageous summer nights. The police were on the defensive, running for their lives. They who thought themselves to be invincible were humbled by a nation of people born into struggle.

Chago

Santiago Villanueva or "Chago" was at the forefront of the Dominican cultural work in the NYC area. A beautiful and serene man, Chago brought smiles to the faces of children and elders alike through his cultural work keeping "gaga" and carnival alive, on boulevards so distant from where these art-forms came to life.[71] Chago was an Afro-Dominican, who wore braids as a reminder that there was no such thing as "bad hair" and that Black hair was beautiful and "good."[72] Adorned with an irrepressible laugh, and deep brown, restless eyes, he was the life of the Tristate Dominican cultural movement. He never missed an opportunity to perform and show his pride in his cultural heritage.

Chago suffered from epilepsy. He suffered bad episodes of epilepsy in which he lost consciousness. On April 16th 2002 he suffered a seizure at the factory where he worked in Bloomfield, New Jersey. The police arrived and instead of offering medical assistance they attempted to arrest him. All of his coworkers were shocked and demanded the police help him. The authorities put him in an illegal chokehold and strangled him to death.

[71] Gaga is a Dominicanized adaptation of *rara*, a Haitian promenade of drumming and dancing.
[72] Reference to the self-denigrating terms "pelo malo y pelo bueno" which continue to be all too common.

Had the police arrived on the scene and found a white man in a similar situation, would they have reacted in such a cruel, inhumane way? Chago was killed because he was Black and because he was an immigrant. Even the courts —notorious for being pro-police— determined that it was homicide that killed Chago. Still, no police officer was ever charged with a crime. Chago was 35 years old. Twelve years later he was still dearly missed. Another generation continued to follow his legacy of learning to love one's self and love one's people in all of their infinite diversity.

"For Balaguer there is a special place Reserved in Hell"

Several months after the murder of Chago, the ancient tyrant, Joaquín Balaguer finally died at the age of 96. Balaguer had served as the ruling class' main political figure and the countries dictator for over 30 years. He continued to run for president even after he was legally blind and suffering from memory loss. When the FALPO heard about his death in the summer of 2002, they felt a dark cloud was removed from the sky. His death coincided with the annual Dominican carnival on Dykman and 204th St. The youth painted t-shirts that read "The tyrant is dead. He'll go straight to hell." Dancing *gaga*, the youth of the MPD wound through the streets, remembering their martyrs and charging Balaguer with theft and murder. Many elder Dominicans were horrified at this response to Balaguer's death. They confronted the rolling Carnival contingent and told them to have more respect. The revolutionary-minded youth respected the elders and let them take the microphone. Dagoberto —almost 65 years old himself— silenced the detractors, citing all of his former classmates who were disappeared for daring to stand up. Upon hearing the agitators assert that "for Balaguer, there was a special place reserved in hell," a polarized crowd became more polarized.

The FALPO distributed thousands of leaflets exposing the dictator's true legacy. The up-and-coming generation felt sad and infuriated to witness a people so colonized and conquered that they admired the very political figures who had disempowered them. Malcolm X warned that "If you're not careful, the newspapers will have you hating the people who are being oppressed, and loving the people who are doing the oppressing." There is so much work that remains to be done.

Toussaint Pacheco

Toussaint Pacheco was among the few young men in all of the Dominican Republic who looked askance at his dual citizenship. He had an American passport but didn't even know where he kept it. Toussaint could have travelled at any moment. He was an American citizen because his father was forced into exile in *los doce años de terror* (the twelve years of terror) and Toussaint was born in Washington Heights, Manhattan. Balaguer's regional lieutenants gave Toussaint's father, Amaury Pacheco a choice: leave El Capotillo with a visa or in a pine wood coffin. Amaury's family rushed him out of the country before he could think twice about it. The division of the family sent his mother into a tail spin. Unable to conceive of being far away from her children, she ended up being interned in a mental hospital.

The MPDista, Amaury settled down in New York but never ceased to be a party militant. Dark-skinned and proud, he never forgot who liberated the slaves of the eastern side of the island in 1822, Haiti. He baptized his Afro-Dominican sons Toussaint and Dessalines, in tribute to the island's liberators.

Every election Amaury Pacheco hoped the blind, old tyrant would finally lose at the polls but Balaguer won five elections and lost none. When the votes were close, Balaguer arrived in a helicopter and brought *fundas* (bags) of groceries for the rural electorate to shore up just enough votes to win every national election. Refusing to extend a truce to anyone that opposed him, Balaguer ensured that hundreds of MPD militants remained in exile, unable to see their families. Balaguer's final victory in 1986, ensuring him power through 1996, was Amaury Pacheco's final defeat. Sick and despondent, the old militant died thousands of miles away from his homeland, in a cold basement apartment, never able to return to his homeland and see his mother in the mental hospital, where she would die.

Toussaint was not going to drown in nostalgia like his *viejo* (old man). He returned to Santo Domingo shortly after his father died, clinging tight to a land to which his father was never able to return. The revolution was a family affair; he prosecuted the struggle in the name of two generations.

When Toussaint graduated from la U.A.S.D., his family urged him to practice law and lead a comfortable life in New York State. But he refused, remarking "If I travel, I'm traveling south. We have Chavez. We have Evo. Those are our brothers. Why would I go north? I'm not chasing their crumbs," referring to the neo-colonizers. "They don't want me there and I don't want them here."

But the movement had other plans for Toussaint. His knowledge of English turned out to be a curse. He was asked to make a two year sacrifice for the party. Short of funds, the vanguard party needed him to go into self-imposed exile and make money to fund MPD activities. He did not vacillate. Within two weeks of the official request, he bought a one-way ticket to JFK airport. When the Central Committee called, a loyal cadre answered. They would inform him when he was to return home.

Newman and Trump

The colonial-imposed reality meant that Toussaint could make more money cleaning toilets in Connecticut than practicing law in the Caribbean. He who swore to never again step foot in *gringolandia* was back two decades after his father's death.

Toussaint's uncle brought him a coat, a winter hat and gloves when he arrived at JFK airport. When he left the Santiago airport, it was 86 degrees. In New York, it was 17 degrees. Steeled from years of aboveground and clandestine work, he was unfazed by the cold. Watching his breath disappear into the stagnant, frigid air, he saw his time in the U.S. as merely another temporary challenge.

There was no self-pity or self-indulgence when Amaury Pacheco was your father.

Toussaint began a job with a landscaping company that serviced the rich suburb of New York, Greenwich. The foremen were white; the laborers were Dominican and Mexican. This was the American dream.

Toussaint never bothered trying to teach Americans his real name and its sacred history; he just told them to call him Tommy. His supervisor's name was Newman, named after the Seinfeld character who was Jerry's neighbor and arch nemesis. Newman was fond of candy bars and marijuana. Every day, the plump, red-necked foreman wore a red "Make America great again" hat. Toussaint wondered when America had ever been "great?" During slavery? Before women could vote? During Jim Crow? By "Make America great again," he understood what was behind Donald Trump's slogan: "Make America great for the rich and the white." But Toussaint was not in Greenwich to win an ideological polemic. There was money to be made and seized. He had received his marching orders and marched to the beat of the collective drum.

The rich family —part owners of the London-based Financial Times and real estate around the world— hired Newman as the caretaker of their property. The partially literate Republican and season ticket holder to WWE (World Wrestling Entertainment) events, claimed the mansion and the properties of the Swiss family, the Scheufeles, as his own personal fiefdom. He rode a golf cart around the estate, shouting orders to *his* laborers and taking weed-smoking breaks every half hour. If other help was too close for comfort, he snuck into an outdoor porter potty to take some hits from his magic pipe. As long as he had his supply of *smidgeons* —his pet name for his weed supply— he was content. The rare moments he ran out, he unleashed his wrath on *his* staff. They learned quick when to stay away from the ill-tempered foreman. But they put up with his foul mouth and white supremacy because they could not afford to bite the hand that fed them. Newman received $50 cash an hour for his services. His help received $40 an hour in theory, but he shaved a lot of that off the top. Nonetheless, cash money for this type of work was hard to come by.

Newman hired "illegal immigrants" to help him because he knew he could "stiff" them and no one would care. His most well-known line was "I'll pay you next week." After enough "next weeks" came and the workers demanded their pay, he asked the hired labor if they wanted him to call immigration on them?

For Newman's lieutenant, work at the Scheufele's estate had its fringe benefits. The Swiss-American family sat atop such a mountain of wealth that they accumulated expensive merchandise, without keeping track of it. Walk-in closets overflowed with designer purses and boxes stacked on top of boxes of Louis Vatton and Jimmy Choo shoes. *Tens of thousands of dollars of shoes for one woman and her daughter?* Toussaint thought, rolling his eyes, thinking the world made little sense to those foolish enough to try to comprehend it. Between the weekly payout, and the shady "benefits," Toussaint was making more money for the party than he ever expected.

As Newman's right-hand man and translator, Toussaint played an important role. Because the jolly, ol' Newman could not get along without him, he let him in on his clandestine schemes. Newman robbed thousands of dollars worth of alcohol, Victoria's secret under-garments and designer clothes, trying to sell them in New York to the highest bidder. The challenge was that Newman didn't have the contacts to "dump the gear," meaning sell the stolen goods for a profit. Again, he depended on Toussaint to make it happen.

The odd couple ransacked bottles of Petrus and Le Pin wine from France and Gianfranco Soldera from Italy. Each bottle had a price tag of $300 or $400 on it. Looking at the bottles with scorn, the Dominican leader could not fathom that a bottle of aged grapes, in a fancy French-labeled bottle, was worth what it would take to bring water to entire streets of el Capotillo, the sprawling slum where his family was from. Toussaint thought of the Burkinabe president, Thomas Sankara's dictum: "How can so few drink champagne when so many cannot access water?" Sifting through dozens of mink coats from Macy's, finding credit cards and twenty, fifty and hundred dollar-bills, the motley crew stumbled on their very own El Dorado. In the blink of an eye, Toussaint transitioned from revolutionary captain to a smuggling captain, but he never lost sight of the end goal. The proud son of Haiti and the Dominican Republic learned from Franklin and other comrades' mistakes. Toussaint knew any day he would transition back to assume his true role in society.

Standing below an intricate Feiss chandelier made of lead diamonds, looking out beyond the terrace at the snow that fell over Greenwich, Connecticut, Toussaint chuckled out loud at the madness of it all. Here he was, a sworn enemy of capitalism, in the very entrails of the beast, alongside a Trump supporter, popping bottles of champagne to celebrate Christmas, in a far off land. If only old man Pacheco was alive to make one more run. The insanity of it all made him laugh, less he cry. He returned to the ideas of Sankara, that treasure chest of revolutionary reflections and experiences: "You cannot carryout fundamental change without a certain amount of madness. In this case, it comes from non-conformity, the courage to turn your back on the old formulas, the courage to invent the future."

Being the assistant to the assistant caretaker of the Scheufeles' estate did not sound like much, but it brought in bundles of cash that Toussaint stored in shoeboxes before sending it off to D.R. Cleaning a billionaire's toilets generated a steady stream of funding that no "legal" hustle could generate. He snooped around closets larger than entire living rooms, expropriating the expropriators. Enrolled as the corrupt *caudillo's* right-hand man, Toussaint made a few thousand dollars cash every week. Every Saturday afternoon, he visited Western Union to send off his dollars to be converted into pesos for the national operations of the liberation movement. For two years, Toussaint played the role of *limpia-letrina* (toiler cleaner). Who would have predicted that Victoria's Secret and Liz Claiborne would fund the revolution?

But according to the laws of physics and dialectics, what comes up, must come down. As quick as Newman built his small empire, everything crumbled before his eyes. The old matriarch's 38 year-old, pampered son, Jeff was notoriously obnoxious. Jeff toke dumps and then refused to flush the toilet. It was his own sick power trip. Toussaint remained unperturbed. He knew Jeff wanted them out of there, purely out of spite. But after a few weeks of flushing the toilet for the haughty heir to a $13 billion dollar fortune, the Trump supporter had enough. Every man has his breaking point and Newman was no different. He confronted the 33-year-old Jeff for his bratty mischief. It was the excuse Jeff was waiting for to call his mother in Geneva. Within an hour, the empress rang Newman. They were all fired. After eight years of riding the Greenwich gravy train, Newman inadvertently bit the rich hand that fed him.

Toussaint was indifferent. He took a $1,500 a week pay cut, pumping gas at a Pakistani-owned service station on Jerome Ave. in the Bronx, staying abreast of the unfolding developments in El Capotillo. A cadre who had been through so many ups and downs, peaks and vallies, only knew inner-fortitude and patience.

Within a few months, Toussaint received a call. The CC was sending him to oversee a cadre school located on the banks of el Rio Osama, the highest concentration of suffering in the entire country. Back in his natural habitat, he facilitated a six month training program for *campesino* and *barrio* recruits. From Greenwich to el Capotillo, democratic centralism giveth and taketh. Toussaint fulfilled his role as a professional revolutionary dispassionately, just as his father, Amaury had taught him.

Mis-leadership: Loose Lips Sink Ships

Constructive critique and internal discipline was an important element of the organizing culture within El MPD. How a group responds to sexist and homophobic behavior among its own members determines how this group will be perceived by the public. Another part of organizing is building alliances with other groups to forge unity.

In exile, in New York City, many of the organizers were young, just coming into manhood. Like Marino, Esteban was one example of a party wrecker who threatened to blemish the reputation of the movement. He aspired to be all things for all people. He had yet to find or define himself so when he announced that he was the self-anointed chairman of the Uptown club of the FALPO, the more experienced organizers were hard-pressed to understand his power grab. Esteban struggled with alcohol and substance abuse and had a bad reputation for mistreating women. When this behavior, contrary to the principles projected by the movement, was allowed to go unchecked, Esteban contributed to dragging a FALPO club with big potential into the ground. Witnessing the downward spiral of this powerful collective, forced young organizers to learn lessons about discipline and organization that would reverberate into the future.

It was the week after 9/11 and New York City was a police state. A group of anti-war activists from the FALPO and other organizations drove out to East New York for a fundraiser for the Sister Soul Project. This was a dance party and there was good revolutionary, anti-war energy. This "leader" made a pass at one of the women from the organization. She did not want anything to do with him. When he brushed his hands over her pelvis, she slapped him across his face. Still, the visual poetry did not cause him to pause and reflect on his behavior. It was sad and hypocritical that this was not the first time this happened. Loyal —perhaps overly loyal because his comrades thought he wanted to genuinely transcend his mistakes— they grabbed him from behind and urged him to calm down. They insisted on taking him back uptown. He was five Heinekens and five shots of Jameson to the wind. Loud and stumbling, he created a scene as the organizers left the community center. One week after the terrorist attacks of 2001, the police sealed off every bridge and enforced checkpoints everywhere. Yet the self-proclaimed "Uptown Chairman" still insisted on bringing drinks into one of the comrade's, Luke's car. Luke grabbed the Heineken out of his grip and smashed it to the ground. Little did he know, Esteban had a few more bottles smuggled under his coat. Fortunately, they made it through the checkpoints and dropped Esteban off.

Ironically, at the 2005 International Youth Festival in Venezuela, Esteban aspired to be the defender of women's honor. He took offense to how Mutassim Billah Gaddafi, the son of Libyan national leader, Muammar Gaddafi, and his entourage behaved towards women. For anyone that knew Esteban, this was truly paradoxical. An international delegate, highly critiqued for his own out of control irresponsible, sexist behavior, took issue with someone else's mistreatment of women? After the two exchanged words, Gadaffi's entourage closed in on him. Esteban looked around to his crew for support. Once again he was on his own. He charged at Gadaffi and was punched out cold by his bodyguards. His nose was broken, bleeding profusely. They retrieved the American flag Esteban carried, which had fallen off to his side during the squabble. They threw it atop his heaving chest and spat on it for good measure.

Not content with one humiliating international episode in Caracas, Esteban returned two days later to add insult to injury. In front of anti-imperialist delegations from around the world in the streets of Caracas, he paraded the American flag around in the closing ceremony of the festival. Delegates from El FALPO and other international delegations questioned his decision to wave a flag under which over 200 invasions of the Caribbean and Latin America were carried out. They confronted him and demanded that he discard the most hated symbol of occupation and genocide. Failing to measure the temperature of his surroundings, Esteban arrogantly brushed aside the critiques and insisted on hoisting the imperial banner up, even as the contingent approached the area where Venezuela's revolutionary leader, Hugo Chavez, was saluting each national delegation. Again, Esteban's beloved flag was ripped from his hands by other youth leaders and tossed on the ground. The timing was impeccable as Chavez, the maximum symbol of oppressed people standing up to empire, witnessed the unfolding of the entire caper.

Deeply insecure, Esteban turned on anyone he considered to be a potential leader in the anti-war and union movement. He embarked on whispering campaigns and spreads rumors that the most talented Dominican and Puerto Rican organizers were state agents. He insisted that everything had to revolve around his calling the shots. With all of his political maneuvering and divisive behavior, the club soon ceased to exist. Why was he allowed to get away with so much inexcusable behavior? His stepfather, Jarvis was a big shot in the American left and Democratic Party, so Esteban was well protected. Jarvis was the Vice-President of the Communist Party USA (the CPUSA). Truthfully the "c" should stand for collaborationist because for over fifty years the CPUSA has been a tail to the Democratic Party's kite. There is nothing communist or respectable about this small grouping known as the CPUSA. They insist that the legacy of the slave owner and slave trader, Thomas Jefferson, and the other founding fathers is "part of working class lineage" and continue to elevate them today as icons to win over the American workers.

What could be more damaging to the integrity of the communist movement than having opportunists and individuals with Democratic Party politics at the helm? Many of the contacts from that period —horrified at what they saw and experienced— drifted away from the movement, some permanently. No amount of damage control could undo the downward spiral this particular FALPO club suffered. Did Jarvis realize he was shooting himself in the foot by protecting his step-son? Who would ever take them seriously? Is the movement supposed to ignore every political folly and abuse and pretend that Esteban was a changed person? Until there was a process of truth and reconciliation, it was impossible to trust "leaders" who had a track record of reckless behavior. The FALPO enforced internal discipline because the very integrity of the organization was on the line. Liberalism, that is letting un-communist and opportunist behavior slide —the very essence of the CPUSA— proved to be political suicide for this branch of the organization.

Coming Aboveground

At the MPD's 23rd national congress, the Central Committee assessed the political situation. They determined that there was too much bloodshed on the side of the people. With Hugo Chavez' successive victories in Venezuela and with all of Latin America on the move, the leadership left behind the burning tires and changed their tactics. They asked: why sacrifice youthful militant energy, when after it was all said and done, there was still a scarcity of water, electricity, ever-rising fares for transport and college tuition and inadequate land and housing? Who was doing all the dying? The most talented sons and daughters of the nation became martyrs, before they had even come of age. Alongside their counterparts in the police, who barely made enough money to feed their families, they died at alarmingly high rates. The national leadership sought to address where the class war headed? 2006 brought a change in

Presidential candidate Fidel Santana
leading a protest in May 2015.

tactics and for the first time in twenty six years, the MPD unfurled the Black and Red flag and flew it publicly. The MPD opened an office off of El Conde, in Santo Domingo's downtown area, and formed an electoral alliance, running Fidel Santana for presidential candidate of the Dominican Republic in 2016. The MPD continues to build unity with other anti-imperialist groups, prosecuting the class struggle using every method available to them. The war is ongoing. In the grand scheme of things, little has changed for the majority of Dominican families, but the resistance movement continues to grow every day.

Jesus Diplan"Chu"
Martyred in 1990.

Rest in Power Comrades

What role models and social model does this system give Dominican youth? Sammy Sosa, Romeo, Alex Rodriguez and Danilo Medina? The youth are bombarded with cliché after cliché —rum, tobacco, baseball, bachata, partying and more partying. The FALPistas were living anti-clichés. For this very reason, they were marked for a double-assassination. Not only were they dangerous in life, they were dangerous in death. Ruling circles acted so that even the memory of their noble, revolutionary conduct was blotted out of the collective memory.

The MPD's detractors will argue that <u>The Saints of Santo Domingo</u> is an over-glorification of their lives. <u>The Saints</u> is not an academic treatise which feigns neutrality. This is a tribute. In a society that suffers from amnesia, I felt duty-bound to remember and write, and then remember some more. Past generations had their heroes, the guerillas of Playa Caracoles led by the Caamaños, Che Guevara's internationalist guerrilla units, the Vietnamese resistance and the Sandinistas. The nay-sayers will spew forth that such ideals belonged to a bygone time. A generation of Dominican fighters continued to revive this very élan. I had rare access to a unique historical personality and world view, one that the dominant class can never squelch.

Premature death has a way of making you pure. How many of our protagonists didn't have time to learn from their missteps and grow? Who would these young women and men have been today, if they were not stolen from us? Why can't we laugh and celebrate life with them? How many lives would they have touched? The figures explored in these pages are legends and the movement today stands on their shoulders.[73] It is not that they were faultless, but the fact that they were defuturized, robbed of a future, in which to grow mindful of their faults. This is the true crime that has been treated with absolute impunity. According to the logic of the Dominican elites, lives that refused to conform, and promised to transform, had to be liquidated.

I grew a great deal politically and ideologically with the generation that inherited the legacy of April 1965, when the Dominican people resisted an U.S. invasion which sought to hurl back the Dominican democratic revolution. What an honor it was to learn alongside selfless, humble warriors what it means to be a MPDista and to follow the legacy of Manolo Taveres Justo, Las Hermanas Mirabal, Maximiliano Gomez, Mamá Tingó, Otto Morales, Jesus "Chu" Diplan and so many other immortal Dominican revolutionaries. These names may not mean much to the reader, but these men and women were bigger than life, the Dominican Republic's version of Malcolm X, Huey P. Newton, Assata Shakur, Martin Luther King Jr. and Stokely Carmichael.

My own humble background, internationalism, political training and love for the underdog positioned me to live alongside a generation soldiers, who will be canonized by history as the fiercest defenders of sovereignty, equality and respect. The martyred take on a mystical character because of the respect that they conveyed for and demanded from others. How large they loomed before the pettiness that presides over the present day order of things, where people are judged for what they have, and not who they are.

Another generation now comes of age that carries their bold, fearless example forward. Ideologically, spiritually and politically

---

[73] Title of an anthology of 365 tributes/poems that I authored dedicated to the ancestors and fighters who came before us.

raised in the spirit of these immortal, self-sacrificing revolutionaries, the FALPistas are "the new men and women" that Che Guevara wrote about. They lay to waste the facile, defeatist claim that all of humanity is confined to a rat race because of our intuitive push towards competition and the notion that all political leadership is corrupt and opportunistic. Youthful, idealistic, and hungry for new horizons, these dogged, young fighters offer us another way to conceive of ourselves and human potential. They were of this society but they soared far beyond it. When confronted with the ruling ideas that drowned so many around them, they rejected them. They didn't opt for a visa to New York or Miami, the lifestyle of a hustler or anything else consumer society tried to sell them. They stood for solidarity, communal ideals and living for others. Their very emergence amidst the hail storm of materialism and individualism —the value pillars of this society— is a testament to the human will to resist injustice. Their integrity and complete surrender to the cause shines out over the Dominican Republic and the diaspora so. Guided by the MPD spirit, future generations will reimagine the potential of the Dominican homeland to liberate itself from the manacles of foreign domination.

To Live Like Them

The reader has been exposed to a radically different view of the Dominican Republic. How much easier would it be to ignore these painful realities and their casualties and to continue to seek out and enjoy the images within the tourist brochures? The MPD understood that the masses of people had the power to sweep away this epoch of dishonor and usher in a day of reckoning with the nation's oppressors. I wrote what I saw and what I lived so that the reader can understand that it is not the revolutionaries who are radical, it is the reality that they combat that is radical. If the saints ignored the deep-seated contradictions and did not seek to challenge them, what type of morality would they be projecting? Is your anger, patriotism and love for life stirred by what you are learning? Denial and fear are two common reasons why people are unwilling to take the blinders off their eyes and confront uncomfortable truths.

"The truth is always concrete," and as long as the immiseration of people continues unimpeded, they will stand up for their interests.[74] Which side will you be on?

The Dominican Republic is the Palestine of the Caribbean. The more resistance fighters who are killed, the more who emerge to volunteer and take their place. When the state strikes down one brave, beloved militant, dozens of others are called to arms to fill the gap. The owning class is playing with fire. And the fire will have the last laugh, just as Quibio, Furi, Caridad and the other saints would have wanted it. Rest in power comrades! We carry you right here in every stone that is launched, in every battered housewife that stands up to her abuser and in every tire that is burned to defy authority. The barricades are erected comrades. We know where we stand. We will be victorious before long!

---

[74] Quote by Georg Wilhelm Friedrich Hegel.

Section II. Supervivencia/Survival

Cárcel Rafey/Rafey Prison

To all of the warriors and survivors
who escaped the silence.
To Emmanuella Odilis:
What can we do
but unite our fears and tears?
Life can only be measured by how much
we sacrifice for future generations.

Escape from Silence

With the sacrifice of innocence
the morning was born.

A would-be assassin's hands were
the forceps of an infant's entrance
Into a planet
Where hope was torn asunder
I was born of rage revulsion and thunder.

They make my world so hard
But I keep on fighting

My insomnia begs for mercy
From merciless nights.
Sleepless
I plead
Please
Can I be reborn?
As a jaguar?
Stealth, outrunning transgressions
Too cold to unfold
As an apparition?
Appearing invisible
Dodging and avoiding inhumanity
Invincible
As an angel?
Flying off and discovering
New beginnings.

They make my world so hard
But I keep on fighting

I dance with the damned
Recite rage with the wretched.
I wander hell
the rungs of my soul
form the underworld
Of a childhood
Devoid
of dancing and dreaming.
Skin scarred by a foreign sin
I'll be damned if I'm consumed within.

Twelve revenants removed from reality
I caress the flames
Redefining insane.
My fury fades into the fiery landscape
Obsessing
My only possession is the perfect
Self-love and outward hatred.

Society underestimated my will to be free
To devour the chains and fallacies
To lay waste to denial and hypocrisy.

I have spent eternal nights
trying to outrun graveyards planted within
Tonight I'm armed with a shovel and a grin.
Trekking towards the source
I dig up the ghosts
From the soil of solitude that inhabits a soul
Accustomed to loath
I explode
through walls and layers of appearance
Scratching away at the essence
Discerning pathological paths
Pointing away from the vortex
I pounce on the curse

of cowardice and emptiness.

These tears go to war
            against eternity
                        against social control
                                    against this troubled world.

                        My life is combat.
                                    Rearing wisdom unborn
                                                Cultivating emerging visions
                                    Harvesting the grace of all children.

I am the protector
                        I infiltrate nightmares
                        I take trauma by his adam's apple
                        I feel him tremble
                        I don't escape
                        I detonate
                        the silence
                        Never alone
                Backed by an army of survivors.

To Eulalia y Yoany: Why couldn't you dance again?

*AIDS is an epidemic that has decimated so many lives across the
Caribbean and around the world. Like all diseases, it affects the
most oppressed communities disproportionately and demands, first
and foremost, not merely a scientific solution, but a social solution.
The Dominican state continues to neglect the conditions responsible
for the ruination of so many young futures. As revolutionaries, how
can we protect our people from this death-phantom? Having lost
people close to me from the virus and seeing how it ravaged my own
family, I wanted to capture the final words a young mother
whispered to me with her eyes when her voice had already died out.
Here I interpret the last thoughts of a 28-year-old mother bidding
farewell to her dreams and desires, before a daughter too innocent
to understand.*

Angelita Negra[75]

My darling little daughter
I remember how cute you were
Cuddled up in your yellow blankie
Stained and worn down
From accompanying us
through so many storms.
How your wide eyes shined out
Illuminating the universe
projecting promise and joy.

What pride I felt
Carrying you in my arms
wherever my destiny roamed.

Soon you will grow into a young beautiful woman
The suitors will come and go
with jewels to entice you

---

[75] Black Angel.

and pretty verses to seduce you.
Don't abandon your village and your home.
Though at times it may seem like nothing,
It's all we have ever had.
All of the simplicity and serenity
temptation can never offer you.

Beware of cunning smiles and promises
Seeking to lure you into their confines.
Cruel daybreaks lurk behind moons
that use the night as a mask.

I couldn't bear to see you trapped
As I once was
With two or three children of your own.
I would screech out in anguish
until I broke the galaxies eardrums

I plead with you
Dare to discover the peace I have never known
Dare to soar through the galaxies where I've never flown.

Mi hija tan preciosa[76]
Don't surrender to hopelessness
Remember all of the flowers
Uprooted from their birthplace
Torn aside and trampled.

Remember the defuturized children
Forced into humiliating corners.
The degradation
Internalized in so many wonderful souls.

Remember your aunts, your grandmother, your cousins
Who were never granted a free stride outside of servility &
submission.
And remember your own mother

[76] My precious daughter

encaged between sorrow and nostalgia.

Carry me with you
Tuck my scars and tragedy
Deep in your memory
So that your passion never vanishes
as mine does today under your breath.

Let me reborn
in your eyes
in your innocence.
We will never look back
We'll ascend high above regret
Coasting through brilliant horizons
gliding atop miraculous rainbows.

Fly away
Keep flying far way
Never look back
I'm afraid this life will swallow you
If you don't escape over the sunset.

You are my reflection
An eternal image of the life I cherished
before I was robbed of a tomorrow.
You are the life that remains faithful,
refusing to abandon these valiant veins.
You are the last tear I will shed
Descending silent and brave
To say good-bye
To whisper one last time
I love you...

Como en toda América[77]

Por los callejones desolados de Puerto Plata
Hermanas nuestras
Mariposas de la madrugada
Bajo la indigna oscuridad
Solo ellas
Y quienes explotan sus endémicos cuerpos
Obligados a satisfacer la dominante imposición
Sobre sus desgarradas rodillas.

Su boca abierta
Dignidad escapando
Auto-desprecio entrando
Veneno goteando en sus gargantas
Sus ojos café
Solitarios
Muertos
Sus mejillas morenas
Llenas de mugre extranjera
De las que se sirve el varón
Presidiendo su cuerpo
Gran dueño de su humillación
Benefactor supremo de sus vidas muertas
Su risa la atormenta
Su carne de tambor
Su propia tierra
Penetrada
Conquistada
Y hecha añicos
Por las manos del caníbal.

---

[77] This poem is about sex tourism, or more accurately sexual exploitation. I did not translate this poem because I could not find the right rhythm in English for it.

A Salomé Siobhan
Por ser indestructible.

Santo Domingo

Frente al amor
Solo sabe susurrar
Sonreír.

Frente al dolor
Solo sabe volar.

To Salomé Siobhan
because you are indestructible.

Santo Domingo

Before love,
you whisper
and smile.

Faced with pain,
you soar.

Section III. Éxodo/Exodus

How many of our people
Cibaeños, Capitaleños, Ayisyen yo
Comparones y campesinos
Tigueres y lo ma desacataos
have drowned fleeing savage seas & history
Seeking this American dream?

Nuestro Middle-Passage pa' Puerto Rico

We've dazed and blazed through continents and centuries
Galaxy-grazing
Moon-raiding
Migrating
Out of shackled skies
But never escaping the master's drooling eyes
that hide
in the blade of the machete
Stocking us through time.
Trapped
The whip's glance beams over our backs
Tracked…

"Coño somebody get her a rag
Esa tipa no sabe
that fresh blood attracts
Death
Wipe that mess up!
She's about to get tossed
Like the last bucket of waste
I'm the captain
And trust me on these seas
A little blood provokes massacres."

"Tranquilo familia. Dejala
If we drown
We go down together

todos juntos
If we make it to Bayamon
We make it together
todos juntos."

"Callate desgraciado
Save your sympathy for when you're in Miami
These sharks aren't' so empathetic
They don't take into consideration
The untimeliness of one mother's situation."

Haaaaaaaaaaaaaaa ..... Splash

Trapped by illusions
Self-hatred
& rum
Here we come.
Tracked by tidal waves
The coast guard
& the sun
Here we come.

Taking to the seas
with nothing more than a backpack
Full of memories
Salami
and american dreams.

Come come
Oye bacan
Before you hit that rum
Pour some out for Paposon
Santo, Damairis and don't forget
El compadre Robertico
Naw mi pana
He ain't drowned yet
But I heard he met this Puerto Rican chick
Dizque he's hopping on the next flight out of Barbaro...
Bound for heaven or hell.

Raised bottles collide
Sending a chill down the universe's spine
This is for all of us who haven't made it
And who will never make it
All of us that will never escape.
Escape!
Escape!
If we were a race of angels that could fly
Only the dust, chancletas y burros would stay behind
Under these evicted skies.
Tragando polvo y desempleo
Loco pa' arrancar lejo'.

Maybe one in a thousand has a chance
Shhhhhhhhhhhhhhhhh
Listen to the waves nestle into their trance
You can hear the leftovers and litter atop them dance.

The refuse
That refuses to be refused
Slaps our ancestors across the face
Between hambre & exodus we're never safe.

Silent pleas
splash up against the bones
Stacked neatly in rows
Mocking our route
for the modern day capital of the Caribbean
Miami.

"Are we there yet?
We been out here for a solid week
Those that ain't vomiting up la tripa from the stale bread
Are peeling out our eyes from staring down the sun
Ha and they want to know why we come
Because there's no where else to run
So Babylon here we come.

Listen to the ocean's echoes
Follow the bones
Follow the bones
Mocking the route towards a tomorrow
deprived of a today
so despite the amores y niños we just can't stay.

{-El Viejo Martire rises from the front of the yola}

"El pipo! Que lo que me pueden decir a mi, mi hijo?
I buried my own daughter
With a kiss and a shovel.
We had to ration the tears
Because down here
In Santo Domingo
We can't afford no more.
Just a glimpse of Manhattan's skyline
is the closest I've been to free.
So these seas better fear me."
These oceans know me
We are on a first name basis
"Dame Luz Martire"
So stagnancy is the basis
You can't feed your family so you flee
What am I but another veteran sea-warrior
7th time I fled to the seas
every time locked down by sailors and marines.
Manaña it's back to the same black outs and latrines
Que se joda! Next time I'm not bringing my dreams.

I breathe
Entre una pesadilla and a dream
Not this time mi hija
Deported back to reality by la guardia
$15,000 pesos round trip to get shipped back to la patria
Aqui estoy en la mismo hoya
Worth the same dead or alive to my familia
Fuck it!
I'll be back defying fate on these seas mañana."

Ambiorix told me this story before he was deported. He almost died in an "yola" (speedboat) trying to get to Puerto Rico then Manhattan. Then he almost died trying to survive here. He told me he felt like he died 900 times when they threw him in jail. He died so many times, he forgot he was alive. When he was shipped back to his homeland, he died from the humiliation. He had only one thing on his mind, how to repeat the journey. Trapped in a time machine, tossed back and forth between illusions and hopelessness, Ambiorix shared this image from his second passage over.

Ambiorix y Dios[78]

Déjame decirte gringo[79]
There is nothing beautiful about the waves
when seen from this side of the cosmos.
We got tossed so high we got a peak at *Dios*[80]
Me being polite, I said Hello.
He just stared at me
He had beer cans all around his throne.
He burped and winked at me.
I swear gringo
I saw God midflight
and he could have cared less about our plight.

That's why I mock this heaven
Invented
By stomachs staring down lonely plates of *guineos y rulos.*[81]

My vision was betrayed by traitorous nights

---

[78] Ambiorix and God
[79] "Let me tell you white man"
[80] God
[81] Two staple foods that are types of bananas that can be boiled. They are meant to be served with meat or eggs but in the homes of the poor, sometimes they are accompanied only by some corn oil.

And mini-wanna-be-dwarfed-Christs
who reign over our lagrimas[82]
Preying on our fears
Plundering our prayers
Gobbling up our blood sweat and tears.
Snoozing and boozing
Your God was no different
than the rest of this sick version of humanity.

Sabana de la Mar
1998

---

[82] Tears

Wake up, run a few miles,
drink a smoothie, put in work at the boxing gym.
This was my routine for so many years.
I came across so many great minds in my journey.
But so many creative spirits were crippled by a lack of work.
I wrote this to capture some of those images
that came to me one jobless, dream-filled day.

500 Trinity Ave.

Stories that make the streets weep
Souls so mean
they make the concrete bleed.

Tears shed   in solidarity with soldiers never
born
and niños[83] never reared
abandoned by broken villages
That stand as islands   scattered across
barren asphalt seas.

Me and Boo Boo Smooth stroll down 1 3 8
slowed up by bygone principles and truncated strides
Fractionalized
in constant contradictory motion
I cease to seek
and retreat to sleep.
Partner: I'm afraid I can't help you find a way out
because I have yet to find an escape myself.

Me and Smooth cut across St. Mary's park
Relaxed
Geared up for 24 laps
We come upon a familiar scene

---

[83] Children.

some bad ass thirteens
out to pounce on the more vulnerable teens.
IPods, bikes, scooters are all up for grabs.
We spot the local crew
Next thing you know we are in pursuit
I try to track down and weave together
Elements of an untold history and misunderstood reality...

Of fire hydrants that have turned their backs on children
Leaving little tempers to sizzle over the concrete
attacking little *manos*[84] and feet.
My people wield scars
As swords
and tears
as razors.

I'll explode on anyone
Who mirrors my own reality.

We head back up 1 4 9
Smooth sees his man Mingo.
Now Mingo was once a peaceful drunk
A proud superintendant
Today he wanders Jackson
trading war stories with the wind
lashing out at on-looking children
He dresses up in painter's pants
and pretends to go out looking for work.
Shunning the sun
He punches in with a concealed bottle of rum.
A cantankerous soul
Tucked deep away in the shade
Cursing out the inevitable arrival of another day.

Dignity is
on a crash course
to turn on itself

---

[84] Hands.

and in a moment of self-loathing
lash out
and leap off the tracks of the 5 train.

We bounce to Burnside
We peep Jaina and her crew
19 years pregnant with despair
Inhaling more smoke than sustenance.
Ecstasy and envy
permeate the pours of an unfeeling asphalt
Hide a baggie of bliss
Under a rat's whisper
stay high for 30 minutes
Followed by the dehydration of your senses
For lifetimes to come.

Now Lorena estaba buena
pero mira ahora[85]
Crouched over before her kids on 180th and Creston
Pleading with the pavement
To rub away the absence
Oh shit look at her roll in the oblivion
We gather around
Mocking one of misery's many marvels
Anxious to gawk at another's tears
When we been turning the same tricks year after year.

Welcome to the blocks
where people don't leave
Unless they're taking the 4 train to 54th and Lexington
to clean the offices of yuppies, bluppies & pruppies
More than happy to give 30 cent raises
to those who never complain.

Me and Smooth roll to Orchard Beach
Its July 4th but this year we never made it past the entrance
Traffic was backed up across the Cross Bronx

---

[85] Lorena was fine but look at her now.

so we celebrated our Dependence on the BX 12.

86 people flesh to flesh on one bus
all in new bathing suits
that a year later still haven't been broken in.

We stumble upon Gunz Smack
Time to grab a snack
For $2.25 you can clog your arteries
for the length of upcoming centuries.
and if you can't afford the public transportation
you get tagged with a $125 ticket
where for every social worker or well intentioned teacher
the system trains bands of C.O.'s, pigs and snitches
paid to fill quotas
of young Black and Latino prisoners.

Me and Smooth keep walking
Searching for an image of a hero
as we trod over the fallen herds of homeless.

The Bronx
Where for every politician spewing out non-sense
there are 100 warriors who say fuck politricks
where for every absentee slumlord getting rich
there are families waiting on food stamps and WIC
where the trains, hallways and elevators
all reek of a common illness
Hope drenched in absence
where plastic coats the sofas
because we were never really here.

We hit up Walton & 183rd
Where Mr. Goldfarb
Never shows up
Unless there is a Section 8 complaint
Of a defiant Dominican Doña[86]

---

[86] Señora

Who divided up her living room and kitchen
To rent out every square inch of her existence.
To every last one of her relative's relatives.

Where every month is eviction season
Three days to relocate or everything is seized.

Where we have healthy kin-competitions
To see who can fit the most family in one apartment
Fifteen people in a two bedroom is the local mark
Though it's not listed in the Guinness book of world records.

One mirthless morning it dawned on me
The whole East Coast was conceived in our image
Paterson, Bridgeport and Baltimore
Camden, Newark and North Philly
and everywhere else there are Puerto Ricans, Blacks,
poor white trash, heroin and crack
Bombed out buildings and heaps of rotting trash.
Miami's Tractor-Trailer park projects
of Hialea and Opa Locka where every nation
in Latin America and the Caribbean
is represented in a 100 yard radius.

The Diaspora of the Forgotten
Swept under a coast-to-coast carpet
Like rats we escape to scurry
But don't worry
there is always one of our very own
to keep us down.
Amen to Imperialism
It has a certain way of bringing us all together
It's just too bad we can't find ourselves.

500 Trinity Ave. Apt 6G
July 4th 2002.

A Day in the Life

Bronx Steam of Consciousness

Bronx Family Court, the Child Support Division. Mothers wait from 8 a.m. until 5 p.m. just for a future court date. Fathers swoop in — cutting the line— hoping they can bribe their former companions with cash money. The Welfare Office. The lines, the bickering, the heat, the gossiping, the fear, the crying babies, the snitching. The office floors -disinfected and bleached- reek of silenced stories and truncated beats. Bronx Lebanon Asthma Center, a half-day's pay for a doctor from New Jersey to tell you your son has asthma because of the environment he lives in. The Agency of Children Services. Four suburban men in ties decide that young children are better off confined in an old, indifferent foster "parent's" apartment than with their own mother. New York City Housing Authority: ten years waiting for an apartment. WIC (Women, Infants, Children), The Methadone Clinic, Medicaid. Federal Plaza: where we line up for passports y *ciudadania* to forget our birthplaces y *patrias*.[87] Car insurance in another state and in another name because we can't afford the $200 dollar monthly rate. We have so many phony addresses that sometimes we forget where we're going and where we are coming from. Mental Health Services where you only get a therapist if you can prove you are going to hurt someone. Lincoln Hospital the Trauma Ward: where teenage patients are handcuffed to the beds. Food Stamp updates. Every day is swallowed by appointments and new obstacles. An appointment to make an appointment to remind you of your next appointment to reregister for dependency and make sure you are still poor enough to collect crumbs.

The police stroll in droves knocking on project doors. Everyone is a suspect. The surveillance is omnipresent. Social security plots pit *familias* against families in income tax schemes. Paddy-wagons erase blocks and their memory underneath a rat's heartbeat. Parking Tickets are worth two day's pay. Every block is regulated. 73 year-

---

[87] Citizenship and homelands.

old judges hand out sentences and ethics hammered out in alien epochs to the descendants of share croppers and indentured servants.[88]   The Adolescent Remand Detention Center, Riker's Island.   16,000 youth are in decay before they ever even had the chance dream.   One social worker for every one thousand Black and Latino children locked up in prison.   One warden and five CO's for every fifty children.   The South Bronx: where jails, projects and high-schools trade kids on the open market.   Unemployment lines & three hour phone conversations to prove that yes I have to depend on my enemy for my survival.   The police commissioner's cars crisscross 149th St. and Jackson.   They convene in the parking lots of projects to hang out talking about 'this is the best show on earth.' Loitering in your own building, urinating, trespassing, hopping the train.   We elbow each other in line fighting for our constitutional right to pay our fines first.   One man throws down his stack of papers, the other lets his bible drop.   It comes to blows.   The rest of us just observe from the line, afraid to break it up because we might lose our place in the queue of slaves.   We are so at war with ourselves we have no time to wonder who put us here.

Only the early bird gets a seat on the train of wage slaves, headed downtown to pick up after lazy rich men who can't pick after themselves.   Others stay behind.   Crack rocks rolled up in tin foil under air conditioners and garbage cans.   New Pentecostal churches and a liquor stores sprout up on every corner.   Feigned insurance scheme crashes get grandmother's killed by accident.   The greasiest of grease sold two for a dollar.   Routine is the whip-cracker.   Roses and peaches can't sneak through the concrete but bushels of escapism are guaranteed.   Seven year olds throw 'fart bags' in your window if you leave it slightly cracked.   When they hit ten, they line you up in the scope of a BB gun.   Project elevators coated with a layer of antiseptic against the backdrop of urine, saliva and filth. The rusting steel windows.   Delusional Roach Syndrome.   In the countryside families, await the milkman's weekly rounds.   Here the exterminator is never late.   He is the bearer of good and bad tidings and any local weekly update.

---

[88] A Mexican worker falls off of a roof to his doom. Afraid to make a complaint, his coworkers leave him in the project courtyard.

They obliterated our heroes then they obliterated our very memory. A strict regimen of self-control. The meticulous crafting of a self-contained world. If they already tapped your mind, why do they need to tap your phone? Any creative whim has already been sucked up by the specialized state administration. The shadowing of every impulse. To deprive us of anything that might spark resistance, to encircle us with the never-questioning civil servants. The compliance and obedience. Hundreds of thousands of clogs in the machine —overseers— mediate the interaction between the two worlds, that of the native and that of the invader. The case workers, the well-intentioned, naive middle-class teachers, the lawyers, the bailiffs, the judges. Strict and masochistic. Strictly sadistic. Every agent has a minion. Every assistant a lackey. Every politician an appealing speech. Flunkies' flunkies. Junkies' junkies. Sister against sister. Brother against brother. One class lives off of the imprisonment of another.

The invasive state. Every day a new layer. The bureaucracy is so thick; you can no longer hear the city's heart tick. We vent our hate and resentment inward, disciplined to stifle dissent. The game is to scurry and to gnaw to come out on top of somebody, of anybody. As long as I'm not at the bottom, I am better than someone. The South Bronx has so many cages, we can't see how we're compartmentalized and blinded, before one grand confinement. And this is a day in the life of the Bronx's impenetrable state bureaucracy.

Dedicated to Dagoberto, Mayito, Monica, Fidel, Higinio
& todos mis padres y mentores.[89]
Para mi pana Pedro Pietri[90]
Again in 2015 they came
and ain't a god damn thing changed.

Dominican Obituary

In a far off distant land
they prayed
and prayed
and finally they came.

They came.
They assimilated
into barrios donde se habla español[91]
because Donald Trump wants them asimilados[92]
as long as they don't assimilate into his neighborhood.

They came.
They got lost on the N-train
They came.
Ashamed
to ask
"Jew spik tha englis o espanis?"[93]
They had to borrow a phone to call uptown
"Primo estoy perdido en Queens."[94]

They came.
to care
for other people's children

---

[89] All of my parents.
[90] For my partner Pedro Pietri
[91] Into neighborhoods where Spanish is spoken
[92] Assimilated
[93] Mispronunciation of Do you speak English or Spanish?
[94] Cousin: I am lost in Queens!

as la esquina
y la calle[95]
raised theirs.

They came.
they were disgraced
when they arrived five minutes after eight
because the train delivering the slaves was late.

They came.
Danilo spent his birthday
in Quisqueya Telephone Agency on 153rd.
It was the third year in a row he bought a few six packs
& downed them solo swearing he was going back.[96]

They came.
In seven years they never learned their neighbor's names
afraid of crossing project hallways
and taking the elevator with strangers
They came
unable to escape.

They came.
For nine years they never complained
shuffled around by the employment agency.
They came
to slave
for $4.15 se fajan every day in factories.[97]

They came.
but we never cared
if they needed a break
after 11 years of cleaning up
after you and me.

---

[95] The corner and the streets
[96] alone
[97] They work hard

They came.
Supervised by a routine
Franscisco
Lucresia
Felix
Eladia
Alfredo
y Mercedes
who spent the night of the millennium alone
speaking to photos
of her husband and three hijos.[98]

They came.
They spent Christmas in an Uptown basement
gathered around the telephone
listening to the operator
"Lo sentimos
Todos los circuitos estan ocupados
Trate su llamada mas tarde Codetel."[99]

They came.
They sang
the same hymns in la iglesia[100]
but every Sunday their Catholic voices grew fainter.
They came.
They brought their grandchildren with them everywhere
to every appointment
Nine-year old translators more experienced
than anyone working for the United Nations.

They came.
They waited
for a visa for mamá.
They waited

---

[98] Children.
[99] Recorded message saying that all of the phone lines are busy and a call cannot be completed at this time.
[100] Church

for a visa for papa.
They waited for residencia
They waited in the emergency room
from 11 p.m. to 5 a.m.
but no doctor ever came.
They waited
and waited...
They waited on you.
They waited on me.
but we never asked
if their smile was real or fake.

They came.
They felt pain
because they couldn't communicate
with their own sons and daughters.
They signed up for English classes
After eight hours on their feet
They came.
Drained
"E' que esa vaina no me entra"[101]
They practiced with the mirror
but desesperanza was their only reflection[102]
Discouraging their noble efforts
"Dejese de esa vaina
maldita lengua pesá"[103]

They came.
Eternally afraid
that NYCHA would find out
that two families were staying together in that one apartment on
Trinity Ave.

They came.
to save.

---

[101] This English stuff I just can't get it.
[102] hopelessness
[103] Give it up. Your tongue is too heavy.

What a fantasy!
They came
They spent $100 a month on phone cards
and sent the rest home to family.
They came.
and saved
so that they could one day have some place to call home
They saved a few thousand dollars over sixteen years
Where is the rest?
ask Con Edison
pregúntale a AT&T[104]
ask Metropolitan Transit Authority
or the owner of the bodega
ask Lincoln Hospital
but above all
ask the landlord.

They came.
and spent a night in jail
for trespassing in their own building
where they had lived for seventeen years.

They came.
They never decorated
they never got a Christmas tree
because they were never really here.

They came.
but their smiles remained
in the pores of the land
they refused to abandon.

They came.
Their parents disappeared
but they weren't there
to deliver them to the next world
because the consul wouldn't give them a visa to go back home.

---

[104] Ask

They came.
They prayed
maybe Dios was too far away to hear.[105]

They came
and year after year
They swore next year they were returning.

They came.
to where they were misunderstood, judged and hated
They came
but through all these years
they never changed.
They remained more humble and resilient than ever.

They came
They prayed and they prayed
but aquí in this strange foreign land they silently died away.[106]

---

[105] God
[106] Here

Mortuorio Dominicano

Ellos rezaron y rezaron
Y por fin llegaron.

Llegaron
A cuidar niños ajenos
Mientras que la esquina y las calles criaron los suyos.

Llegaron fueron regañados
Porque llegaron cinco minutos después de las ocho
Porque se atrasó el tren de los esclavos.

Llegaron
Nunca se quejaron
Movidos por la agencia del empleo
Llegaron,
Se esclavizaron
Por $4.15 se convirtieron en robots del norte.

Llegaron supervisados por una rutina
Francisco
Lucrecia
Felix
Eladia
Alfredo
Y Merecedes
La que pasó la noche del milenio
Sola hablando con fotos
De su esposo y tres hijos.

Llegaron
Cantaron los mismos himnos de la iglesia
Llegaron.
Y cada domingo su voz cristiana
Se turnó mas estropajosa

Llegaron

Esperaban
Por una visa para mamá
Y otra visa para papá
Esperaban por la residencia
Esperaban y esperaban
Esperaban en la sala de emergencia
Pero ningún medico vino…
Llegaron
Y siguen esperando.

Llegaron
Para ahorrar
Pero que gran mentira!
Llegaron
Y lo intentaron
Gastaron $150 mensual en tarjetas telefónicas
Mandaron lo demás a sus padres
Llegaron
Ahorraron
Solo $5,000 dólares a través de 16 anos
Lo demás?
Pregúntale a Comp. Edison
Pregúntale a AT&T
Pregúntale a Metropolitan Transit Authority
Pregúntale al pulpero de la esquina
Pregúntale al viejo barrigón de la farmacia
Pero sobre todo
Pregúntale al casero.

Llegaron
Pero nunca pusieron arbolitos

Llegaron
Pero nunca estuvieron aquí de verdad.
Porque sus sonrisas se quedaron
Allá en los poros de la tierra que dejaron.

Llegaron y desaparecieron
Pero no hubo nadie para llevarlos al otro mundo

Porque a sus familiares le negaba la visa el cónsul.

Llegaron a rezar y rezar
Pero here in Manhatten
Se quedaron.

The following poem is in Haitian Kreyòl. It is about the Haitian immigrant experience in Flatbush, Brooklyn, N.Y. I have included it in this anthology because of the commonalites in the Dominican and Haitian immigrant experience.

Sa se pou tout konpatriyòt
ki pèdi nan Nou Yòk
K'ap bat dlo pou fè bè
kap chèche yon rèv ki pa janm ekziste.

Zantray Ayisyen

Yo te priye
Yo te priye pou chape
Mèsi Bondye
Yo te rive.

Yo te rive…
Nan ti katye Flatbush
Yo te rasanble
Pou pale ti kreyòl yo
Paske blan meriken vle boure kilti pa yo nan kolèt yo
Toutotan se nan lakou blan y'ap drive.

Yo te rive
Nan tren nimewo de yo te pedi
Se pa ti wont, yo te wont mande polis yo:
"Msye eske ou pale franse?"
Yo rele yon vye kouzen *colect* nan Brooklyn
"Patnè mwen pèdi nan Manhaten."

Yo te rive
Nenpòt kijan
Kit se nan ti bato
Kit se nan avyon sou dekolaj
Men yo pa ka trouve lavi miyo

146

Si yo toujou sere pou imigrasyon.

Yo te rive
Vin fè tchoul pitit blan
Tandiske ti pa yo
Leve nan kafou ak lari.

Yo te rive
Andre te pase jou fèt li
Chita sou yon vye chèz nan *Teleko*
Li te pale avek cheri li
Depi twa zan se konsa
Fwa sa se ra se ta…
Li pwomèt tèt li
"M'ap retounen lakay mwen"
Bon pa bon
Wè pa wè
Lakay se lakay.

Yo te rive
Sa gentan fè setan depi
Yo rete nan vye bildin nan Church Ave.
Men se pa sa ki fè yo konnen kijan vwazinaj yo rele
Yo te pè
Flannen nan koridò bildin nan
Lè yo pran asansè
Yo frikat.

Yo te rive
Men yo pat ka chape poul yo, po dyab.

Nevan gentan pase men yo pa jamn plenyen
Biwo travay voye yo nan tout kalite djòb dezonè
Blan yo te fè yo travay tankou bourik
Ap fèmen zye la jounen kou nan nwit pandan onzan
Ap ranmase fatra nan tè etranje.
Yo te mande lanmò
Nan djòb sal $4.15 dola pa è nan faktori
Yo travay kon satan.

Yo te rive
Polis yo te flanke yo nan prizon
Pou tèt yo te antre nan yon bildin dròg
Kote yo te rete pou disetan.

Yo te sou kontwòl
Nanm yo, Lespri yo, ata kè yo te sou kontwól
Se woutin ki se sipèvisè pa yo
Jan
Mari
Claude
Fatima
Gladis
Ak Filome
Ki te rive
Pou vin swadizan fè ekonomi
Pou ede lòt ki dèyè
Se pa ti manti!
Li te rasanble $3,000 U.S. pandan trèzan
Men kote tout lajan sa yo pase???

Mande AT&T
Mande Metropolitan Transit Authority
Mande King's County Emergency Room
Mande mèt boutik nan kafou
Sitou mande mèt kay la.

E Pòl?
Ki te vini pòv nan depanse
Senkant dola chak mwa nan kat telefòn
Ti sa ki te reta a
Se te pou voye lakay
Paske lakay pa bon.

Yo te rive
Pil sou pil
Yo te kwè se te syèl poutan se te lanfè
Tout moun pou lan demil la te avèk fanmi yo

Nan reveyon genyen ki nan bato
Nan restoran e nan bal djaz.
Se te avèk tristès mwen te wè Yvon
Li menm te akoupi devan de ti foto dè Madame li ak de pitit fi li.
Li te menm pale avek foto sa yo.

Yo te rive.
Yo te kite peyi yo
Kote tout fanmi yo te renmen yo
Pou vin viv nan yon lòt sosyete ki refize asepte yo
Men pandan tout ane sa yo
Yo pa janm chanje
Malgre tout bagay sa
Yo toujou rete Ayisyen.

Yo te rive
Men yo pat janm la vreman
Yo te kite gete yo
Zantray yo
Nan demanbre lakay.

Yo te rive
Men yo pat gen denye priyè
Paske pitit yo pat ka wè yo avan yo ale nan syèl
Paske konsil la te refize yo viza a.
Yo te rive
Men Bon Dye pa te tande yo sipliye'l
Petèt ki te sere twò lwen
Nan tiwa kay gran blan
Paske here in Brooklyn
Zo yo te rete
Men Nanm yo te tounen Ayiti.

La Plenn, Potoprins
21 Mas 2001

Every generation receives a nickname. "The Depression Era Babies, The Baby Boomers, Generation X." Who makes these names up? No one ever consulted us. Like everything else to do with identity and definition in this society, it was hurled down on us. But Generation X? What a meaningless, disorienting name!

Come Chill with the chants
Supplicated from castrated lips

Generation Lockdown

We are...
Born into the descent.
Recruited by the social order's wardens
In the pre-birth stages of development.

We are...
The products of the politicians' counterfeit smiles and rhetoric.
Hatched from a pipe and syringe
Left to trickle into the hands of our interrogators.

We are...
Fastened in the system's grip.
Squirming
Clenched.
Dragons bound to explode
Left to corrode.

We are...
Thunder lynched.
Sovereignty swaying beneath the same rope.
On a treadmill sprinting towards a new beginning
Trying to outrun Rockefeller's glance
We were born without a chance.

We are...

Silence
Desiring to rumble
The reminisced
Begging to be relived.

We are…
a people without a homeland.

We come of age in a trance
In which red white and blue symbolize innocence
Rikers, Sing Sing
Angola, Marion
Exiled in our own land.

We are…
Convicted
Lives that function as static statistics
and fit the government's definition of delinquent.

We are…
Oversleeping
Desperate for a mission.

I haven't heard an alarm clock in two years
I roll over at 3 in the afternoon
And no one gives two shits.

We linger on the inside
Struggling to lift
muzzles off minds and lives.
To pronounce Biko's unfinished verses
To converse with our lineage
To join
Our ancestors
Whose fists grip
the bars erected across our vision.
We are…
Unbroken
Verses left unspoken

Vilified
Denied jobs
Denied life.
I'm not here for what I did
I'm here for who I am.
The politician's election strategy for dealing with unemployment.

We are…
The commodities necessary for "progress"
Filling up coffins
Laying before headstones
At a profit margin of seven digits.

We are…
The correction officer's pension.

Faith's afterlife
Seized and sentenced
To death by lethal injection.

We are…
The youth tossed into hell
Bound to rebel.

For Ariel and all of our people
Abducted
Languishing in the Prison Industrial Complex.
Disappeared
Out there somewhere
Consumed by the shadows
in search of the sun.

Exiled into the Forgotten

The concrete bars spring up & spread
across the globe
Weeding out the scoped and the scopers
The doped and the copers.

Here we grown men dwell
Piled up in a cell
where soft is a synonym for deceased
and reason exists as a luxury.

.

Riding the tension between weaklings and beasts
Buried alive among *puñeteros* and Jesus freaks
My pen and pad rise up and spit my history.

Exíliame hacia mi tierra
Exíliame hacia mi infancia
Depórtame hacia mis raíces
Yo Nací libre
Que diablos hago yo aqui?

Do you know how it feels?
To wake up and turn your back to the sun
Because money is so sparse
you survive crumb by crumb.
So this sleep is on
Arch enemy of the dusk and the dawn
Condense four more hours into a mili-second

And I'm gone…

Fading away…
…Fading away
Embracing the shade
But another stranger to the day.

I'm assed out
So I can't back out
95 South's the quick route
to come up on some sweet loot
My chance to rise & shine
and kiss these undocumented woes goodbye.

They said this shit would be *lo màs facìl*
Transport ecstasy interstate
They never mentioned the rats and the raids
the cuffs and the cage.

Who thought Pololo the *chivato* would snitch?
Roaches rat out their own cousin for a nickel
Bitch-ass snitch-scum
Stole away my smile, my skies, and my son.

You see our dreams
Have always been faithful patriots
Whirling past project skyscrapers
Elevating beyond the rat's & roach's gaze
Migrating South to escape
But most of our vacations are upstate.
Attica, Bedford Hills, Greenhaven
En Riker's *La Roca* rotting away
Open up the coffins
Sparford, Bronx House
Watch my sovereignty hop in
Coxsackie, Clinton, Sing Sing
Where liquid dreams
Run rusty
Solidified into

concrete nightmares
Erected
In two million lost glares.

We've been surviving on our own
For much too long
We've been taken for granted
For much too long.

Undressed by the undertones
of death's echoes
Marion, San Quentin
Soledad, Folsom
Leavenworth, Angola
Tear all the bricks down
Raze all the pain.

Pack my *maletas* & I'm ghost
Northbound *amargao*
Chained and shackled down
A phone call away from oblivion
Bienvenidos to your new home!

Now I'm stored away in this cage
En la casa del diablo
Hibernating
in permanent mind vegetation.

Coño I won't see the block again on Intervale
Until I'm too old to make love again anyway
So why second-guess death?
If my universe is condensed
Into an hour glass that doesn't tick…

Aquí estoy
In search of the sun
Exiled into the forgotten…

Devuélveme la vida
Just Let me be

Freeing capacity
Realization
Un-leash Me me me…
Yo Nací libre
Que diablos hago yo aquí?

I feel the ghosts
Challenging to vanquish my sight
Robbed of six years in my prime
My memory slips
Nearly resigning

Sighing I seek to subside
Focusing in on Yasaira's wide-Brown eyes
Sentient but numbed
Two human emotions away from suicide
I stroke…
My first human contact in a month.
Ejecting self-pity and strife
Releasing a sign of life…

The satellites of imperial foresight
visualize and extradite
this mass exodus towards death.

Where are all of the Patria's Soldiers?

We wander Washington Heights
Wallowing amidst the memories
of vecinos, morir soñandos[107] y peace
Outrunning resacas[108] and the police
Talking about who we used to be?
And who we're going to be?
But who are we?

We are
The dueños[109] of our own ruin
Oh to consume your own doom!
Clinging to our necks
Cluttered in our living rooms
Consuming! Consuming!
Doomed to be Doomed!

Nosotros somos[110]
the owners of corners
where coronas and dominos devour hours.
Amaneciendo[111]
Kickin' it
Addicted!
to bull- shitting
& General Tsao's chicken.

---

[107] Neighbors, Dominican milk shake made out of carnation milk, orange juice and sugar.
[108] Hang-overs.
[109] Masters
[110] We are
[111] Breaking night

On these streets where experience
is your savior
Extracting lovelife lessons from the pavement
Survival lesson #1:
Don't drink on the lonsome
Dos: Date tu basilon[112]
Pero nunca bregue sin un condon[113]
Last but not least
Don't fall into too deep of sleep
You might wake up
On the other side of eternity.

Caught in the thick
Of inverted galaxies
We lust for the future
Sin haber analizado el pasado.[114]

Swallowing &
Inhaling!
Trying to set out sailing
Over a horizon too arrogant
to even give us a chance
so we mindlessly dance
to a rhythm we no longer control.

You can see us on 207th and Dykman
Conversing with midnights
Riding the breeze of weed
Migrating through locked centuries
& lost hemispheres
On to esquinas[115] where time doesn't exist
& sueños[116] have been kidnapped
Their necks slit &

---

[112] Enjoy yourself

[113] But don't have sex without a condom.

[114] Without having analyzed the past.

[115] Corners.

[116] Dreams

slashed
as the blood slithers through the cracks
left to drip
on concrete
that never really gave three shits.

Nosotros estamos posted up on blocks and stoops[117]
Privando en bueno[118]
Tragos trickle down throats like veneno[119]
Escuchando dembo
Piropiando
de largartijas pa'ribba
Toda falda aunque sea una escoba
Dale pa' bajo
puros sicopatas
que venga lo que sea
Sobreviviendo
piratiando como un desgradiado
todo lo que se ha inventao
Yerba, videos y romo.
Jangiando y tripiando
Prendido, rulay en coro[120]

"Diablo loco, en Santo Domingo
te acuerdas cómo
ligamos todas esas jevas
y te acuerdas de mi carrito loco.
Andábamos nítido por toda la Capital"[121]

Gripping each presidente like it was a memory[122]

---

[117] We are
[118] Showing off
[119] Shots of alcohol trickle down our throats like poison.
[120] Clowning around and commenting on all the women who pass by. Every female and any female. Get it. Pure psychopaths. I don't care what happens. Surviving. Hustling like a motherfucker everything that has ever been invented. Weed, videos and rum. Hanging and partying. Lit up with my crew.
[121] Fuck bro, you remember how in Santo Domingo we got all the girls. You remember my whip bro. We were chilling out there.

acariciando botellas como si fueran doncellas
Nostalgia
transports us back in time
send home some clothes & gold that shine
and we swear we're progressing
But la verdad es que we're[123]
Chillin!
Standing
stationary
Visionless
Stagnant
Caught up in the enemy's labyrinth
playing with out own breath
battling los nervios y el frio
"Coño si yo pego este numero!"[124]

Sigh after sigh
Año tras año
Seguimos roamin' this warped time zone[125]
Known as Uptown.
Fanáticos del Patrón del Mar
El Chivo, El Capo
y mil otra novelas[126]
Any mechanism for our minds to flee
Scattering before police and sleep
Hiding in junkie's hallways and callejones[127]
Wondering if we were meant to be
God-damned by destiny?

y la vaina que más me quilla[128]
is that I'm living their dream.

---

[122] Dominican national beer

[123] The truth is

[124] Battling the shakes and the cold. Damn if I don't hit this lottery soon!

[125] Year after year we keep roaming...

[126] Big fans of soap operas

[127] Alleyways.

[128] The shit that fucks with me the most

Millions will voyage to the seas
Abandoning patria[129]
Dying...
to be...
... me.

---

[129] Abandoning homeland

Section IV. Historia y Horizontes/
History and Horizons

Maximiliano Gomez "El Moreno"

Cimarrona

My memory is a minefield.
I track back detonating distrust & paralysis.
Every second is a love-life lesson
Life lived as a rebellion
Eluding echoes and ghosts
of a survival demobilized by chains and posts.
Cognizant of the fault lines
Between love and revulsion
I drift out of the spectrum
Reinventing the dimensions
of continents and redemption.
Centuries past &
Hemispheres trespassed

My mind is still in mutiny.
Reminiscence and memory
are the captives who refuse to obey orders
begetting strife and disorder
revolting on a violent vessel left stranded
to navigate the depths of naked nights
striving for the right to life...

My night vision floats over the ocean
sovereignty lives in motion
my calves and mind permanently flexed
storms flee a mother's flesh.
Pain resurrected in my voice is sedition.
I hurl lightening under my breath as the wind
gathers and listens.

Mamá Tingó

The tyrant lynched the night
Hunting her step.
She refuses to rest.
Her cry
Never sleeps
Giving birth to
Mountains…
Resisting.

Mamá Tingó

Linchó la noche el tirano
Cazando sus huellas
Ella se niega a descansar
Su grito
Amanece
Pare bosques
Montañas
Y resiste.

A whisper discovered by Guajiros[130]
Read, analyzed, understood

Assata

Conceived by the Taínos
Descendent
of the tense muscles of the *mambises.*
The maroons' sea shells and the machetes
rise from your chest.
The braids of all of the Americas
born of Africa
flow from beneath your beret.
Your roots emerge
from a port in the Congo
an auction in La Habana Vieja
a tobacco plantation in Virginia.
Momentarily wrenched from their homeland
They stopped growing.
Today they are reborn within you
In your freedom gaze
Illuminating the future
with all the power of an insurgent past.
Bartolina Sisa

---

[130] Cuban word for peasants. The backbone of the Cuban revolution.

Mamá Tingó
Domitila Barrios de Chungara
Haydée Santamaría
Sing within you.
Reunited by anguish
by rage.
They gather around a stream
for an internal moment.
Their silence purifies the water
that reach out to the Americas.
Once damned up by old slave masters
The winds pushed them forward
A tidal waves that overwhelmed and engulfed slave ships
Repopulating the Sierra Maestra
Your sacred habitat.

Assata

Susurro descubierto por guajiros
Leída comprendida y liberada

Assata

Formada del taíno
y los músculos tensos de los mambises.
Los escudos y las lanzas cimarrones
surgen de tu pecho.
Las trenzas de toda América
paridas por el África
fluyen por los bordes de tu boina.
Sus raíces
colocadas
en un puerto del Congo
se subastan en la vieja Habana
para una plantación de tabaco en Virginia
Por un instante arrancadas de cuajo
dejaron de crecer.
Renacieron en ti
en tu mirada
relumbrando hacia el futuro
con todo el poder de nuestro glorioso pasado.
Dentro de ti cantan
Bartolina Sisa
Mamá Tingó

Domitila Barrios de Chungara
Haydee Santamaría
Reunidas por la angustia y la rabia
de un segundo eterno
alrededor de un arroyo.
Purificando el agua
Preñando las cordilleras en un poema
que antes de llegar al oído de las Américas
fue encendido por un viejo amo de esclavos
pero el viento la salvó
deslizándola sobre barcos negreros
que la llevaron a la Sierra Maestra
su habitad sagrada.

Assata

Sebastian Lemba Calembo was the herculean leader of the 1532 slave rebellion in the Dominican Republic.

Lemba

On a sweltering tropical night, in a plantation tucked away somewhere between nightmares and homeland, stern chains began to soften and confide in his flesh. Beneath the overconfident laughs that beamed out of the big house, hundreds of shackled whispers spoke to his worn marrow, vowing a different ending. Though inclined to silence and reserved in speech, Lemba was forever attentive to every detail of bondage. He had collected the whip-cracker's secrets and weaknesses, in preparation for a twist to the master's dénouement. And like that –in a matter of seconds that stood up as centuries- the humidity and the whip were broken by unified machetes and a final silence.

The French slave master Duclos complained that Jean Jacques Dessalines wasn't like the other slaves on Haiti's sugar cane plantations. With panic in his eyes, he stated that this African was unique, for being "the hardest-working of the beasts but also the most disobedient of the dogs." His premonition was correct. The slave by the name of Dessalines would go on to change the very course of history and haunt the serenity of the slave masters for centuries to come.

Dessalines

As the other slaves continued in their trance
He devoured midnights and danced.
The uneasy breath
of fallen spirits
wouldn't allow him to drift
into the valleys of sleep
nestled away neatly
torture & tears
miseries & luxuries.

Bathed in mists of redemption
Insomnia was his only companion.
He crawled out of the slave quarters
To hide deep down in the dawn

With arms extended
and continents connected
He inhaled the advent
Receiving strength from the rain
pledging his people would rise again.

Across the ocean he smuggled visions & dreams
That his mother once bathed at the foot of hot-springs
Detached from the source
He composed fresh roots and tongues
With all the motives to loath
He poised potions of vengeance with love.
While remaining motionless
He advanced breath by breath
Sigh by sigh
Creeping over the earth
Conscious that one sound
would be his demise.

The scheme slithered
through the maze of grins and graves
Whispering under vigilant breaths
Slipping beneath window sills, gates & excess
His glare entranced chandeliers and fate
His razor-sharp tears tamed the tongues of traitors.

Chains caressed the chubby cheeks
of the master's children
As the beloved but mistrusted rocked their cradles
to the cadence of calmed calamities.

Guided by calloused hymns
And neglected wisdom
Young minds were uplifted.
Transported through agony and time
into the heart of blood-stained seas
and into a future of unknown memories.

Their preparation

Continued with exact discipline
Until one sinister hour
a servant stumbled upon the encounter.
He tried to sip from the sequence
But the milk was too sour.
Always faithful to reason and civilization
He alerted his governor.
Squealing he tried to launch his screams
But it was not as destiny would deem.
His silence was the last melody of
the slave cradle-song
and the first verse of a new dawn.

Greedy grins
were the kindling
for flames
fueled by failed fates
Flowing full circle
Reviving
lost smiles and rituals.
Stones marched along side
Boomerangs
Abducted by abuses
Too cold to unfold.
Axes came home to roost
Ascending with poised pitchforks
Calm and cold-blooded
where courage was thought to have been castrated.
Baptized by Black fire
An army of machetes saluted the sky.

Oliverio Mateo, or Papá Liborio was the leader
of a peasant movement in the
Dominican Republic against the US occupation.
He was murdered in 1922 but his ghosts
haunt the occupiers to this day.

Papá Liborio y los Gavilleros

Toiler
of tempests
and agony
He resisted
Cornered
in the veins
Of the deep south
Palma sola
Extends into the skies.

Jornalero
de tempestades
y angustias
Desafío
atrincherado
en las venas
del profundo sur
Palma sola y su cielo.

Jacques Viau Renaud

The dawn
rises
Defying anguish.
Uniting
The thirst
The tension
Hopes
Of two people
Undivided.

El alba
se levanta
Desafiando la angustia
Uniéndose
En la sed
La inquietud
Y la esperanza
De dos pueblos
Indivisibles.

Coronel Francisco Caamaño[131]

A master of history
A servant of the future.
He wore the breeze
as a bullet proof vest
Before he could be silenced, his audacity shot on the ambush.
Before he could be extinguished
He distributed smiles and confidence.

Today if you walk those same beaches and mountains
where legends once exchanged silence for thunderclaps
If you concentrate long enough
You can hear his laugh and
see his smile sketched across the skyline.

73 moons later Playa Caracoles remains pregnant
With the winds of the future.

---

[131] In February of 1973 Caamaño led a guerrilla expedition of Dominican revolutionaries trained in Cuba to oppose the dictatorship of Joaquin Balaguer. He was killed on the 16th.

El Coronel de Abril
Coronel Francisco Caamaño

Rostro que refleja la historia de la sangre
Siervo del futuro.
Llevaba la brisa como un chaleco a prueba de balas
Antes de que pudiera ser silenciado, su audacia disparo en la
emboscada.
Antes de que pudiera ser extinguido
Repartió sonrisas y confianza.

Hoy en día, si usted camina esas mismas playas y montañas
donde las leyendas una vez intercambiaron silencio por truenos
Si te concentras lo suficiente
Usted puede escuchar su risa y
ver su sonrisa esbozada a través del horizonte.

Algunas lunas más tarde
Playa Caracoles queda embarazada
Con los vientos del futuro.

*This is dedicated to our brother and friend, Chago
from the world of rara and gaga, happiness and freedom.
Chago was brutally stolen from us
by the Bloomfield, New Jersey police in 2002
because he was an immigrant and because he was Black.*

Santiago Villanueva

Chago Chago Chago

Return to our side
Black lightening.

Chago Chago Chago

Maroon
Born of bodegas and bateyes
Resurrected in the ideas of Tupac when he sings
In the braids of Bob Marley when he meditates
Redeemed
By the flames of the drum
Spreading love and heat
across barren seas of concrete.

Chago Chago Chago

Black lightning
Unleashed
On hate

Black lightening
Revived
in the density of your pain
in a city addicted to silence.

Querida Familia:
Esto es un poema que dedico a un compañero nuestro
que fue asesinado por la policía
porque era un inmigrante y porque era negro.

Chago Chago Chago

Santiago Villanueva

Chago
Retorna del silencio
Con un grito

Chago Chago Chago

Cimarrón
que se redime
en el fuego del sudor
En los ojos del tambor
En los rieles de Harlem
En los talleres de sudor del Bronx
los batayes de Paterson
En la epilepsia de Bloomfield
Asesinado

Chago Chago Chago

Relámpago Negro
Suelto
por las sendas del opresor
Relámpago Negro
Suelto
en la densidad de tu dolor.

Chago Chago Chago

Redimido
en la voz de la bodega y la bandera
en la lengua de Tupac cuando canta
en las trenzas de Bob Marley cuando medita
en los puños de Tingó cuando combate.

Chago Chago Chago

Te escurres…
en la mirada
de una ciudad
adicta a este maldito silencio.

Juana Colon

She cultivates daybreaks
and commands the skies.
She makes it hail rocks and fire
over strikebreakers and supervisors.
La bandera de sangre[132]
can never silence her
Lies will never invisibilize her.
Those who pillage her land
can never appropriate her history

---

[132] The flag of blood.

Juana Colon

Aparcera del rocío
y del verde ancho
de la hoja del tabaco
que entre granizadas de piedra y fuego
sostiene la hoguera de la huelga
Jamás podrán silenciar tu grito
Jamás podrán invisibilizar tu cielo
y liar la historia del pueblo puertoriqueño.

Dedicated to my paisanos:[133]
Lori Berenson and Ben Linder
to all the orphans of the north
who have never felt like gringos
nor acted like colonizers.

Paisana

Deep down the shadows of the jungle
Scattering seeds across the sunset
Protecting children from foreign winds.

Within the reflection of Tupaj Amaru
The future mounts

---

[133] Countrymen/women

your restless bravery
outrunning and outmaneuvering the CIA
With happiness and bravery.

There you are
Eternal
Kneeling
atop the sun's surface
in a stream
Pure
Scrubbing a pan
And scrubbing away the pain.

Orphan of the north
Adopted by America
Baptized in Peru
with your own sacrifice
And the blood of silence.

The blood
that today erupts
in the veins
of indomitable volcanoes.

My paisana
Proud of the homeland
That you have cultivated
In my consciousness.

A Lori Berenson
y a Ben Linder
igual a todos los gringos que:
se han desgringoizado
y no se sienten ni actúan como colonizadores

Paisana Mía

Dentro de la sombra de la selva
regando semillas a la gloria
arrancándole los chavalos al viento.

Encima del reflejo de Tupaj Amaru
montando nuestros niños
en tu bravura inquieta
pateándole el trasero
a la CIA con tu alegría.

De rodillas
en la superficie del sol
en un arroyo
desnuda
fregando una paila.

Huérfana del norte
adoptada por América.
Bautizada en Perú
con tu propia sangre
que erupciona hoy
por la venas
de nuestros volcanes.

Paisana Mía
orgulloso de la patria
que has sembrado en mi alma
con tu lucha.

Section V. Unidad/Unity

Originally published in Liberation newspaper April1, 2011.

Dominican Government Continues Repression of Revolutionary Activists

By Daniel Shaw and Gloria Lazarro

Freedom for Braulio Vargas!

Another leader of the Dominican Popular Movement, Braulio Vargas, of Navarrete, was recently sentenced to 20 years in prison. Vargas is the most recent victim in a 55-year campaign of repression by the state to destroy the MPD, the longest standing Marxist-Leninist organization in the Dominican Republic. Despite the state terrorism, the MPD continues to oppose imperialist intervention, the exploitation of natural resources by transnational corporations, and the oligarchy's domination over the immense majority of Dominican workers and peasants. Throughout its long history of state terrorism and corruption, the Dominican government has received the economic and military backing of Washington.

Building up the Police State: The Aftermath of Invasion

In 1965, the U.S. government invaded the Dominican Republic with 42,000 troops in order to repress a popular rebellion against the dictatorial government that aimed to restore the democratically elected president, Juan Bosch. After two years of US military occupation, U.S. military personnel stayed to train the Dominican National Guard and State Police. The hated, foreign backed government was determined to destroy any organized opposition to the regime of the Reformist Party. The corrupt elections, again overseen by the U.S. government, placed Joaquin Balaguer into power from 1966 to 1978.

This period of Dominican history is popularly known as "the 12 years of terror." Balaguer's state police executed more than 3,000 leaders of the MPD and other left parties. This covert war resembled COINTELPRO's efforts to destroy national liberation movements in the United States. Fearing repression, leftists were forced to operate clandestinely; study groups would rip the covers off of communist literature so as not to be spotted reading forbidden material.

In 1961, the national office of the MPD was reduced to ashes by Trujillo's police and paramilitary forces. U.S. intelligence unleashed a public relations campaign to defame the MPD throughout Latin American as declassified Pentagon documents have shown.

Under the cover of the Cold War, the CIA set up operations in DR in order to infiltrate the MPD with the goal of taking out its leadership. Dan Mitrione, a CIA agent, helped set up the *Banda Coloradá* death squads.[134]

Amín Abel, one of the most brilliant and charismatic youth in Dominican history, was assassinated at 28 years old. Abel had led the struggle for open admissions for working class students at the first university of the Americas La UASD (La Universidad

---

[134] "The Red Gang" referred to the color of Balaguer's Reformist Party

Autónoma de Santo Domingo). The police shot him to death in his home in front of his family.

Maximiliano Gomez "El Moreno" was born to a peasant family in the impoverished province of San Pedro de Macoris. Gomez was forced to drop out of school because he could not afford shoes to go to school. Possessing a humble demeanor, a great command of Marxist theory and an unwavering commitment to struggle, El Moreno was elected the Secretary General of the MPD in 1966. The MPD freed him in a hostage exchange for State Department Colonel Donald J. Crowley, but in 1971, he was poisoned to death in Brussels while in exile.

Numerous other revolutionary leaders were assassinated: Otto Morales, Amaury Germán Aristy, Roberto Figueroa (Chapó), Tito Montes, Henry Segarra Santos, Stalin García, Juan Pablo (Pelayo) Félix.

All were veterans of the Dominican people's war against the 1965 imperialist invasion and students and practitioners of Marxism. Though the Dominican state stole the lives of an entire generation of bright and brave youth, preventing them from taking their rightful place among their people, other leaders emerged and the struggle for a worker's revolution in Santo Domingo continued.

The FALPO (Broad Front of People's Struggle) faces state assassinations

The revolutionary generation of El Moreno has inspired the present-day generation to continue the class struggle in the factories, the countryside, oppressed communities and in the streets. Forced to go underground, el MPD organized a popular front in the oppressed neighborhoods throughout the country called "el FALPO." The greatest weapon of the workers, peasants and unemployed has been direct struggle with "the general strike" used to shut down entire cities.

The demands of the FALPO have been access to basic services, electricity, running water, education, health care as well as an end to the drug trade and government corruption. Risking their own lives,

Braulio Vargas and other leaders of the FALPO have led this decisive struggle. The Dominican police, trained by the Miami and New York City Police Departments in military combat and counterinsurgency, gunned down dozens of the FALPO's youth leadership.

Youth leaders such as Jesus Rafael Diplan Martinez "El Chu," Yito Gomez, Junior Espinal, Elvin Amable Rodriguez "Ony", Osvaldo Torres "El Fury", Jonathan Duran, Jose Aquiles, Jose Rodriguez among others have been shot and killed in cold blood by the armed forces.

As the leader of the FALPO in Navarrete, Braulio Vargas demanded a popular tribunal to try the local government for the misuse of public funds. Vargas openly denounced the systematic theft by the mayor Amantina Gomez and brought to light the role Mayor Gomez played in the drug trade. The FALPO also has a campaign demanding that Law 176-07 about Participatory Budgets approved in July of 2007. This would mean the community itself would determine which public works to prioritize and the mayor's office has to publicly announce how the city's funds are distributed.

After waging this campaign, Vargas was persecuted, subjected to raids of his home in the middle of the night and forced to go underground. Finally captured and imprisoned on trumped up charges, Vargas' trial was filled with inconsistencies, with corruption and open intimidation revealing its political nature.

The state is hoping to send a message to the revolutionary movement as a whole: you will be killed or put in jail. But the people have refused to cease their struggle.

Repression Breeds Resistance

According to the World Bank, nearly half of the Dominican population continues to live in poverty—although the real figure is likely be even higher. Without economic opportunities in the countryside, millions of families have been forced to flee to the cities. Without a place to live, they build makeshift homes from zinc, wood, cement blocks in neighborhoods that have no urban planning, employment, education nor basic services. Sixty percent of the population lives in urban encampments without any escape from poverty. Basic staple foods prices continue to soar. School breakfasts have been suspended.

Because of the widespread suffering and unemployment, foreign capital is able to set up "Free Trade Zones" as the only source of work. These sweatshops which produce everything from Fruit of the Loom, to Timberlands to Tommy Hilfiger only pays $70 for a fifty-hour work week. Now the Free Trade Zone workers are also encouraged to bring their piece-work home in order to sew more clothes.

For opposing this economic exploitation, the leadership of the left has been assassinated during strikes, physically incapacitated, and illegally incarcerated. But the revolutionary forces continue to fight on the road towards victory, today more determined and united than ever.

Despite more than four decades of an uninterrupted war of state repression against the Marxist-Leninist movement in the Dominican Republic, the anti-imperialist movement continues to fight back and grow. From the belly of the beast, the PSL stands with the MPD and all the progressive, anti-imperialist organizations of the Dominican Republic in demanding freedom for Braulio Vargas and all of the political prisoners of the Balaguer, Hipólito Mejía and Leonel Fernández governments.

Originally published in Liberationnews.org in the summer of 2012.

Police Open Fire in Salcedo, DR on a Peaceful Demonstration Killing 4, Wounding Dozens

By Emmanuel Pardilla and Danny Shaw

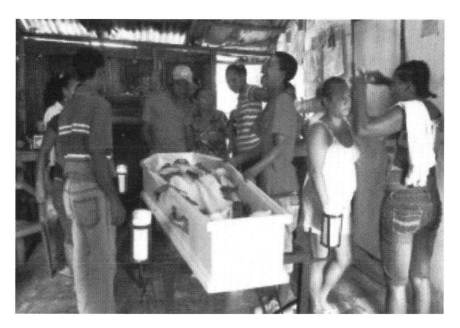

From June 12th through the 14th, the people of the city of Salcedo in the Central North region of the Dominican Republic took to the streets to protest what they are calling the assassination of baseball player and community member Hector Ramon Medina Lopez.

Just a month before on the 12th of May, Medina was fatally shot by the police in the chest while riding a motorcycle with his friend, Cesar Rene Garcia. Garcia was shot in the leg. The police never offered a reason for the shooting. The community's demand for an explanation as to why their beloved son was killed was met with the utmost brutality as the National Police opened fire on unarmed demonstrators killing four and wounding more than twenty. Dozens of others were unjustly imprisoned. One of the more savage scenes caught on tape exposed police roughing up a group of protesters en route to the hospital. Two young men carried a third protester who was wounded by police gun fire in the stomach. The police can be seen stopping the moped, beating the three men and forcing the injured man to walk to the hospital. He died shortly after. FALPO (Frente Amplio de Lucha Popular) leader Dario Camilo outlined the series of the series of assaults and killings of civilians by the Dominican police describing "the brutality as a type of witch hunt against anyone who dares to protest against the government."

Both the Dominican media and the president Leonel Fernandez have remained quiet failing to utter even a word in response to the police massacre. The National Commission on Human Rights (CNDH) has committed 200 lawyers, if need be, to investigate and determine "those responsible for the cruel, inhuman and degrading acts that not only violate the Dominican constitution but are also violations of the Universal Declaration of Human Rights as well as seven pacts and international convents that the Dominican Republic is a party to."

This intense repression follows a consistent pattern of police brutality, intimidation and violence in response to the Dominican people's just outcry for increased social services, a halt to the rising cost of public university tuition and transportation. The state is sending a clear message meant to halt all protest and prevent the unity of different affected sectors of the population. The police violence there is all too similar to the brutality that we suffer here from the Bronx to South Central every day at the hands of the police. The murders of Trayvon Martin and Ramarley Graham are all too similar to the murders the Dominican state continues to carry out. The Party for Socialism and Liberation stands in solidarity with the FALPO and the popular organizations of the DR and their demands for the prosecution of the responsible parties to the massacre from the head of the national police to the president of the Republic.

The War of Faith in the Dominican Republic
The Role of the Church in the Lives of the Poor

Leticia's Story

This past week I was overjoyed to visit my niece Leticia and other family in the Dominican Republic.[1] I had not seen Leticia since she was the ring bearer at my wedding in 1998. She was the cutest little girl imaginable- the perfect reflection of childhood, life, innocence and beauty. But she came from a desperately poor family. The chips were stacked against her from the beginning. I wanted to share her story because it deserves to be told and is reflective of the story of millions of people across the Dominican Republic.

Several years after the wedding, Leticia's mom Margarita died of AIDS. Struggling to put food on the table for her three children, Margarita found herself in debt to the local butcher Miguel Angel and *colmadero* Fausto.[2] She was coerced into sleeping with them in return for the sums unpaid. She contracted the virus. Leticia's father Felix had never recognized her. He was nowhere to be found. Leticia's stepfather Onu sent for her. She left the village of Pontoncito where she grew up and moved to El 27 de Febrero neighborhood. Onu's intentions were good but unemployment and underemployment pushed him into selling marijuana. He found himself in prison. Leticia was again an orphan.

We tried to send for her from New York but bureaucracy has little time for or interest in considering her plight. Leticia had to go back to her village just outside of Navarrete, Santiago. She was raised by her uncle Juan Carlos who did everything in his power to give her the affection and instruction he gave to his own four children. She had another uncle Roberto who lived next door who was an alcoholic and known sexual predator. Sometime between the age of 8 and 9 she was tied down by Roberto and his wife Yuby and sexually abused. How many times was never clear from her conversations with me but it was clear it was not a one time occurrence.

At 12 years of age she got married to a 14 year old *motoconcho* to escape the horror.[3] She was pregnant at 13. A child was left to raise a child. Her own self-esteem un-constructed and dismantled, how would she build up the self-image of her newborn baby Marlenis?

Leticia on April 28th 1998.

Reconnecting

Seventeen years later, the parishioners of her church led me to her doorstep for a visit. She had moved over 200 kilometers away to los Frailes II, a peripheral neighborhood of Santo Domingo. Her mouth was agape and tears surfaced in both of her eyes when she realized her uncle had tracked her down after so much time.

Here was Leticia before me –pregnant with her third child- renting a room with her husband who had been deported from New York City because of involvement with drugs. The petite little 6 year-old now weighed 225 lbs. This cruel life had taken its toll on both her mind and body. Penniless -but keeping with tradition- she mustered up some change to offer my son (her cousin) and I some grape soda and cookies. How could one decline given the sacrifice and pride it took to offer up the *merienda*?[1] She told me about her journey and of her recent turning to God.

Her two-year old son Morocho ran naked perilously close to a steep staircase with no rail. Out of the corner of her eye she saw her nine-year old Marlenis playfully chase a neighbor's daughter around. Whack. She slapped her in the back of the neck, bestowed curses upon her and returned to the righteous theme before us. She told me all of the tragedy and catastrophe we are seeing in the world has been predicted. "It is all explained in the bible. Ebola, the war in Jerusalem, the earthquake in China, the poverty in Africa." She explained that this is what her pastor says.

I asked her about her husband and how their marriage was going. There had been a lot of violence and she lost a pregnancy from the force of some of his blows. She said his behavior has improved since they joined the local Evangelical church.

An afternoon onslaught of rain began to pour down. Left with no toys or space to play, Marlenis created fun out of nothing and ran around the two-room hovel. Again a mother's impatient hand struck down on Marlenis' head tossing in "*a maldita prieta*" for good measure.[2] Like Leticia, Marlenis was the darkest-complexioned in the family. It seemed like the harshest life sentences are always reserved for the darkest children. Taught to hate themselves, they hate that which most closely mirrors their own pain.

Finding a Purpose in a World that Makes Little Sense

With so many of my family members "finding" themselves in God, I wanted to reflect on this all-too-true social reality. Every day more people are further distanced from gaining control over their immediate surroundings and fall deeper into superstitious beliefs that an almighty being will make things better. Across Latin America, from Santo Domingo to the Bronx we hear that Jesus is coming and that everything will be ok. The German poet Henrich Heine speaks to the fact that religion for the poor is a comfort where there is no logical reason to feel comfort: "Welcome be a religion that pours into the bitter chalice of the suffering human species some sweet, soporific drops of spiritual opium, some drops of love, hope and faith." After all when all people have known is tragedy, don't they need something to believe in? Everyday more and more Evangelical churches pop up in our *barrios* and *campos* absorbing the time and energies of our social class.[3] The churches' continued success is the continued failure of their alternative; social organizations that can re-channel the energies of the dispossessed.

Revolutionaries also have an iron-clad belief that another world is abloom. Diametrically opposed to spiritual idealism, this world view provides explanations for the most simple and complex social phenomena. If the revolutionary forces of the Dominican Republican were winning the war of faith, the multitude of barrio and campo inhabitants would line up to hear a different analysis of shifting world events; the displacement of the Palestinian people, the centuries-long underdevelopment of the African continent, the white-supremacist media's obsession with disease, famine and Africa and the colonial earthquake that left Haiti vulnerable to a natural disaster in the first place. Imagine if they were then positioned and empowered to throw off the restraints of poverty. Who could be against that goal?

The pastors and churches play a very important role in diverting the energies of our social class into the blind alley of surrendering power to the almighty. Forking over their destiny to the omniscient, they cease to be self-determining. This view is not synonymous with a blanket condemnation of all religions. Independent of one's spiritual faith, one can be a fighter and defender of humanity. There needs to be unity with anyone that is willing to organize against the structures that oppress us. Latin America has given countless examples of fighters who emerged from the church...Oscar Romero, Ernesto Cardenal, Camilo Torres and so many other practitioners of Liberation Theology. A resurgence of this type of socially-committed congregation could challenge religion as it is being taught by the dominant church who intentionally foments dissociation, a disconnect between cause and effect.

The Institutionalization of Hopelessness

It only makes sense from the logic of this system that every corner of an oppressed community would have a church, a place to play the lottery and a liquor store. These three social institutions -parachuted down upon the poor- are three types of booze that disempower us. Lenin -reflecting in 1905 on the role of religion in the lives of the Russian peasantry- writes the following:

"Religion is one of the forms of spiritual oppression which everywhere weighs down heavily upon the masses of the people, over burdened by their perpetual work for others, by want and isolation. Impotence of the exploited classes in their struggle against the exploiters just as inevitably gives rise to the belief in a better life after death as impotence of the savage in his battle with nature gives rise to belief in gods, devils, miracles, and the like. Those who toil and live in want all their lives are taught by religion to be submissive and patient while here on earth, and to take comfort in the hope of a heavenly reward. But those who live by the labour of others are taught by religion to practice charity while on earth, thus offering them a very cheap way of justifying their entire existence as exploiters and selling them at a moderate price tickets to well-being in heaven. Religion is opium for the people. Religion is a sort of spiritual booze, in which the slaves of capital drown their human image, their demand for a life more or less worthy of man." [4]

Local "bank" where residents play the lottery. Many youth work in these "banks" earning $1,250 pesos or $29.50 a week for over 50 hours of work which requires them to work on Saturdays and Sundays as well.

Alienated by this concrete world, the oppressed search for and retreat into other imaginary worlds. "Religion is the sigh of the oppressed creature, the heart of a heartless world, and the soul of soulless conditions."[1] In Revolutionary Suicide, Huey P. Newton writes: "My opinion is that the term "God" belongs to the realm of concepts, that it is dependent upon man for its existence. If God does not exist unless man exists, then man must be here to produce God. It logically follows, then, that man created God, and if the creator is greater than that which is created, then we must hold that man is the highest good." A people's religious fanaticism is a direct measure of their social alienation. Dreams -stagnated and frustrated- remain stubborn and take off nonetheless, but into orbits alien to their own interests. "Serving God" becomes a raison d'etre for those who feel meek and un-emboldened by material reality. Newton calls this " the tyranny of the future" (179). The hope of heaven and fear of hell demobilize people. The "I am weak and though art mighty" mentality only helps those in power.

And here before us is a strange God indeed. Witnessing the triumph of greed and exploitation, wouldn't God summon us up off of our knees towards action to free ourselves from this condition? "Less singing and more swinging" as Malcolm X put it. If Leticia and her social class believed in one another and their capacity to organize together for change as fervently as they believe in the ever-after, how invincible would the toiling classes be before their oppressors?

The church's existence and towering presence in the lives of the poor is no coincidence. As missionaries are lauded as heroes, revolutionaries are picked off and beheaded. Just in the "twelve years of terror" of dictator Joaquin Balaguer, 3,000 Dominican leftist leaders were assassinated for daring to defy dictatorship. Of the generation I came of age with in the anti-imperialist organization *El Frente Amplio de Lucha Popular*, dozens are dead, others paralyzed from the waist down, others in exile, still others languishing in the La Victoria and Rafe prisons. Those in power pretend to encourage activism and political engagement but when it challenges their stranglehold over power, they strike back with vengeance.

The Central Question before Us

If the world is awash with abundance –of water, of agriculture, of resources, of land, of life- why then do so many children suffer? This is the central question for any student of Dominican studies or any of the social sciences. Our people have been left with no way of understanding the cruel machinations of power and inequality. Christianity and other organized religions explain this all away. We are collectively being punished for our lack of faith, or so the reasoning goes. Evangelical minister Pat Robertson's comments about the earthquake in Haiti being a consequence of Haiti's lack of Christianity and his insistence that "we need to pray for them a great turning to God" reflects this racist mode of thinking. If Robertson had ever spent time in Haiti, he would know that Haiti is a country of great faith. Some ethnographic studies estimate that 80% of Haiti practices Christianity.[2] For no one prays harder and more than the poor. If faith and praying were to earn a nation freedom from want, Nicaragua, the Philippines, Ireland and so many other "good Christian nations" would be paradises on earth.

A revolutionary then is a relentless atheist, looking deep into history and science in order to explain all social phenomena. This is not to say that we do not have our own private beliefs or faith. I cherish and depend on my own spirituality and connection to nature to endure the doldrums of everyday working existence in New York City. But my world view does not pivot on spiritual faith alone. I believe in myself and I believe in my people. To wrench power away from its thieves and restore it back to the Leticias, Margaritas and Marlenis…this is the mighty task of immeasurable faith that is before us. If your congregation fails to understand this, then who are you serving?

Endnotes

[1] Marx, K. 1976. *Introduction to A Contribution to the Critique of Hegel's Philosophy of Right*. Collected Works, volume 3. New York.
[2] Farmer, Paul. The Uses of Haiti.
[1] The names of the survivors have been changed to protect their privacy. Only the names of the sexual predators remain unchanged.
[2] Owner of the local corner store where foodstuffs and toiletries are purchased.
[3] Motoconchos are motor-taxis.
[4] Light afternoon snack.
[5] Dominican term meaning good-for-nothing Black girl, all too often used against dark-skinned children.
[6] Novaya Zhizn No. 28, December 3, 1905. First legal newspaper of the Russian Social Democratic Labor Party.
[7] Marx, K. 1976. *Introduction to A Contribution to the Critique of Hegel's Philosophy of Right*. Collected Works, volume 3. New York.
[9] Farmer, Paul. The Uses of Haiti.

Originally published in Liberation School on February 27th, 2016.

What Does the 27th of February Mean to me? Behind the Mask of Dominican 'Independence'

By Graciela Pichardo and Danny Shaw

The Dominican Republic is the only oppressed country that celebrates its "independence" from another oppressed, colonized country, Haiti. For generations, the fear-mongering, racist Dominican ruling class has deliberately manipulated the history of the two countries, particularly the period between 1822 and 1844, in order to perpetuate *el anti-Haitianismo* (anti-Haitian racism). The truth is that Haitians have never been responsible for the inequality and the dismal socio-economic conditions that exist in the Dominican Republic. Imperialism and a handful of elite families — the Vicinis, Bonettis, Barcelós, and Brugals, among others— who drape themselves in the Dominican flag and engage in a shamefaced, rhetorical admiration for Duarte, Sanchez y Mella, *los padres de la patria* (the fathers of the homeland)—are the true usurpers of "Dominican independence."

The facts behind Haiti's Unification of the Island

The Haitian slave revolution of 1804 —overcoming seemingly insurmountable odds—was one of the great achievements recorded in human history. Hundreds of thousands of former slaves waged a popular war that defeated successive French invasions under the command of Napoleon Bonaparte (James 1938). After the former slaves, turned generals, Toussaint L'ouverture and Jean-JacquesDessalines mobilized the Haitian people into a formidable fighting force, never again could the naysayers proclaim that revolution and the victory of the most oppressed was impossible.

Having emerged victorious from this sanguinary war of emancipation against the French, that left much of its land burnt to ashes, Haiti sought the unification of the island of *Quisqueya* (the Taíno name, later renamed *Hispaniola*, or Little Spain, by Columbus) as one fortified garrison against recolonization.

There are three incontrovertible facts about the 1822-1844 "unification:"

1) The Haitians entered into the Spanish empire's sphere of influence—later known as the Dominican Republic—because France and the other colonial powers used this colonial outpost to threaten and re-invade Haiti in hopes of re-enslaving Haitians.

2) In 1822, Haiti liberated thousands of slaves in the Dominican Republic and sent former slave owners and landowners fleeing into exile.

3) Upon entering the eastern portion of the island, Haiti expropriated land from the all-powerful Catholic Church and the Spanish crown. This constituted land reform at the tip of "foreign" bayonets, a unique contribution from an "invading" army.

Whereas the Spanish crown built a legal system around the protection of the *encomienda* system, based on slavery and feudalism, the Haitians introduced a legal code that protected all persons of African and Indoamerican heritage. The Haitian constitution —revolutionary in its essence— prohibited foreigners from owning property and extended citizenship and property rights to the humblest social classes. From the point of view of the oppressed, this was the most progressive period in Dominican history (Santiago 2005). From the perspective of the *encomenderos* (plantation bosses), this was an unforgivable intrusion into their profit-making system (Price Mars 1953).

A Nation Divided

Though motivated by anti-colonial principles, the Haitian leadership lacked the economic means to carry out a successful unification of the two nations. Beleaguered by France's enforcement of a "debt collection" of 150 million francs for "lost property" and facing an international blockade, the Haitian administration was unable to respond to the myriad needs of the Dominican population (Moya Pons 1977, Sagás 1994). Haitian President Jean-Pierre Boyer—overseeing 12,000 Haitian troops—faced formidable opposition from Dominican elites who desired further integration into the "global," colonial-dominated economy.

While the long-repressed Blacks and mulattoes welcomed the arrival of an army of former slaves—as a safeguard for their own freedom—the lighter-skinned, propertied *criollo* class saw the "invaders" as a direct threat to their own economic interests and way of life. Led by businessman, Juan Pablo "*el Patricio*" (the Patrician or Aristocrat) Duarte, they conspired and overthrew Haitian rule in 1844 (Ferguson 1992).

The Dominican masses' fears proved to be all too real. With the Haitians now pushed out of the scene after 1844, the privileged *criollos* looked to Spain to re-establish its authority and protect them and their property. The new national anthem of the separatist movement contained the verse "Rise up in arms, oh Spaniards," hinting that this transfer of power was a counterrevolution in property relations. Seeing that its former colony was unprotected, Spain re-implemented slavery. As the word spread among the Black and mulatto population, they revolted against Spanish designs. Santiago Basora was among the newly-freed Black leaders who rebelled against the elitist separatist movement, forcing them, and their colonial overlords, to abandon the idea of reestablishing slavery in D.R. (Torres-Saillant 1998).

In 1861, when wealthy Dominican cattle-rancher and career politician Pedro Santana became the dictator of the Dominican Republic he annexed the country back to Spain, making the D.R. the only country in history to revert back to a colonial status.

The specter of a new era of Spanish colonization and slavery sparked a new nationalist resistance movement. The Black and mulatto masses —led by black General Gregorio Luperón— received support and launched guerrilla attacks from Haiti, successfully defeating the Spanish forces (Torres-Saillant, 1998).

The Centrality of History

History is contested ground. The class forces in power use their own version of history and manipulate it in order to promote myths and advance their interests. The ruling class' "take" then becomes the accepted version of events. The Dominican nationalist version of history paints the western side of the island, Haiti, as a dark, menacing presence that seeks to "re-invade" the peaceful Dominican nation, which must protect itself at all costs. The reality is the opposite; Haitians have been the victims of Dominican state-sponsored racism, forced displacement, and massacres. In October 1937, Dominican dictator Rafael Trujillo oversaw a week-long extermination campaign along the border. Over an estimated 20,000 Haitians were murdered in the "Parsley massacre," and thousands more were displaced.

Haitian and Dominican Solidarity

It is important to highlight the often unknown and downplayed instances of solidarity among the two nations.

As a maroon state, Haiti supported liberation movements throughout the hemisphere. They supported their one time adversary, the Dominican mulatto general, Francisco del Rosario Sanchez, against Spain's next round of encroachments. Simón Bolívar and the anti-colonial movement in El Gran Colombia looked to Haiti for arms and support. The Venezuelan flag was sewn and first flown in

Jacmel, Haiti in 1803 as Francisco de Miranda prepared his anti-colonial expedition to confront Spain. The great Cuban revolutionary José Marti set sail from Haiti when he went to fight for Cuban independence from Spain.

A century before Ernesto "Che" Guevara was born, the Haitians were the original internationalists.

The influence of the Haitian revolution was felt throughout the U.S. The southern slavocracy trembled before the idea that slaves could fight back and win. Denmark Vessey —a slave born in the West Indies and forced to travel to the South as the assistant of a slave trader—led a historic revolt of slaves in Charlestown, North Carolina (Dunkel *Haïti-Progrès September 2003)*. He wrote President Boyer in hopes of expanding the insurrection across the southern states.

During periodic round-ups throughout Dominican history, many Dominican families —risking their own lives— have hidden Haitians who were escaping the machete and gun-wielding military. The 23-year-old poet Jacques Viaux and other Haitians fought and died alongside Dominican revolutionaries in the "constitutional war" of April 1965, resisting the invasion of 42,000 U.S. Marines sent to squash a movement for popular democracy. When Haitians were forced to flee U.S.-backed coups against the democratically elected president Jean Bertrand Aristide in 1991 and 2004, the Dominican solidarity movement received them. The Dominican Republic was the first country to respond to the 2010 earthquake that rocked Port-au-Prince. When the present Dominican government of Danilo Medina passed the law 168-13 in 2013, denying more than 200,000 Dominicans of Haitian descent citizenship, a multinational movement led by both the Dominican and Haitian communities, in the D.R. and the U.S., organized to overturn the law.

Towards Genuine Independence

The February 27th "independence" celebrations are a hollow charade. They are not focused on South-South solidarity or advancing Dominican workers' interests. What plagues the Dominican Republic is not scarcity or competition with another oppressed people, but the greed and opulence of a few, in a word, capitalism.

Dominican elites meeting with Rudolph Guliani

Millions of Dominican workers pour their life blood into the main industries that make the Dominican Republic profitable for investors; sugar processing, ferronickel, gold mining, textiles, cement and tobacco. The Dominican people collectively produce over $101 billion dollars in goods and services every year (CIA World Fact Book country report 2013). From the point of view of economists —and the growth of the Gross Domestic Product— the economy is booming. Yet the average salary for a Dominican worker in these industries is a paltry $850 dollars a year! There is more than enough wealth to satisfy the needs and dreams of the 10.5 million Dominicans in D.R. and those economic migrants forced into exile abroad, including a million in a half who live in the US, over fifty thousand in Spain and tens of thousands of others who live in Puerto Rico, Venezuela, Canada and beyond. But all of the profits are siphoned off to the nation's enemies.

The world's leading gold-mining company, the Barrick Gold Corporation, has billions of dollars invested in extracting gold, nickel and other valuable metals. Franklin Sports, Fruit of the Loom and Adidas owned Dick's Sporting Goods are among the largest exploiters of sweatshop labor in the country, paying as low as an abysmal $32/week or $0.73/hour. Some 378,000 Dominicans work in these sweatshops.

Today's neocolonial profits come on the heels of yesterday's colonial enslavement. Failure to understand this history obfuscates the present moment and leaves the Dominican working class vulnerable to racist dogma of the anti-Haitian forces.

The Dominican bourgeoisie —the junior partners of high finance— strategically focus on a bogey-man, whipping up all types of racist hysteria about a Haitian re-invasion, while genuflecting before the true threat, U.S. imperialism. Hiding behind an imaginary threat, based on a manipulated history, the faux patriots seek to promote their own class interests, callously disregarding the wide spectrum of needs of the Dominican masses.

The Dominican Republic —from its inception—has been a nation divided. There is no united Dominican nation with one set of common interests. While the masses eke out a living that is every day more precarious, the rich continue to play their role as obedient hirelings in the pillaging of the nation. The progressive, anti-imperialist movement calls for unconditional solidarity with Haitians and all oppressed workers and strives to organize the unfinished Dominican revolution so that in a near future we have a definitive independence, worthy of celebration. Until then, everywhere Dominicans reside, in *la patria* (the homeland) and *en exilio* (in exile), la lucha continua/Nou toujou ap lite!

Here is a list of resources for further reading on this topic.

Candelario, Ginetta. "E. B. Black Behind the Ears: Dominican Racial Identity from Museums to Beauty Shops." 2007.

Dunkel, Greg. Haitian History: What U.S. textbooks don't tell. 2003.

Espy, Jay. Advancing the Anti-Racist Struggle in the Dominican Republic. 2015.

Ferguson, James. The Dominican Republic: Beyond the Lighthouse. 1992.

James, CLR. The Black Jacobins. 1938.

Price Mars, Jean. La Republica de Haiti y La Republica Dominicana. 1953.

Sagás, Ernesto. Race and Politics in the Dominican Republic. 2000.

Shaw, Danny. The Saints of Santo Domingo: Dominican Resistance in the Age of Neocolonialism. 2015.

Torres-Saillant, Silvio. "The Tribulations of Blackness: Stages in Dominican Racial Identity." 1998.

Wucker, Michelle. Why the Cocks Fight. 1999.

Venator, Santiago. Charles. "Race, Nation-Building and Legal Transculturation during the Haitian Unification Period (1822-1844): Towards a Dominican Perspective." 2005.

Originally published in Port-au-Prince in Haiti Progres in 2001.

"El Anti-Haitianismo:" An Ideology of Racial Inferiority

Like Palestinians in Israel or Muslims in Bosnia, Haitians in the Dominican Republic are demeaned, harassed, and victimized in both extraordinary and mundane ways. They are subjected to a wide array of demeaning stereotypes.

El Anti-Haitianismo, anti-Haitian racism, is but one symptom of the colonial mind-set in the Dominican Republic. The Dominican people are flooded with intense propaganda denigrating all that is Black/African and glorifying all that is White/European. Many Dominican parents jokingly threaten to send their kids in a sack to a Haitian boogeyman if they misbehave. Haitians are accused of stealing animals, or even children, and sacrificing them. In the mass media, Haitians are identified with hunger, AIDS, political turmoil, and black magic.

Imbued with the myth of their cultural and racial superiority, many Dominicans have turned their backs on Haitian language, history and culture. Popular educators now have the task of reeducating the Dominican population about the Haitian reality and raising awareness of the dangers of anti- Haitian hysteria.

I will analyze just three dimensions of *El Anti-Haitianismo* to show how the Dominican state -whose policies are reminiscent of apartheid- has a vested interest in harassing the Haitian population.

Dominican President Hipólito Mejía's government invests substantial financial and human resources into persecuting Haitians who come to the Dominican Republic. Military checkpoints, one every 15 miles, line the route towards the interior of Santo Domingo. National Guard searches of popular transportation serve to publicly humiliate Haitian migrants and remind them of their status as unwanted visitors to the Dominican Republic. The Dominican military intentionally provokes Haitians by aggressively searching through their belongings, mocking their language, dress, and skin color, and demanding that they pay ridiculous fines. Dominican state police have converted crossing the border and traveling into the interior into a business fueled by bribes and corruption. The most aggressive guards carry out illegal deportations and beatings if Haitians do not give into extortion. Rhetoric about the need to patrol for Haitian arms and drug traffickers serves as the eternal justification for this aggression.

Even Dominican citizens sometimes contribute to this persecution. One Sunday afternoon on a bus returning from the border town of Jimani, I witnessed a young Haitian man being forced from the front to the back of the bus on the charge that he had "el grajo," or body odor. A group of Dominicans waved their hands in front of their noses as if to say that he could not sit close to them. The man was robbed of his right to take an empty seat on a six-hour bus trip.

In counterpoint, the Dominican population is trained to be servile and obedient to German, Spanish, Italian and North American tourists. White Western "grajo" is an afterthought and not a bias permanently attached to their ethnic identity.

The dynamics of "el grajo" is just one element of an aggressive fear of Haitians that goes against the humble nature of the Dominican people and secures their role as the carriers of a necessary racism. "Necessary" because as long as Haitians are viewed as sub-humans, they can more effectively be exploited by international high finance. Racism provides the cloak and justification for their super-exploitation.

The Dominican state apparatus has assumed the leading role in labeling, stereotyping, and scapegoating the Haitian community. The principle figure behind *El Anti-Haitianismo* was former president Joaquin Balaguer, who dedicated his intellectual and literary talents to defaming Haitians. In his book La Isla al Revés, Balaguer stomps vulgarly on the dignity of Haitians, absurdly blaming them for the spread of venereal diseases across the Dominican Republic, among other things. He plays on Dominican society's historical paranoia that Haitians will try once again to unify the two countries under one government as happened from 1822 to 1844. Inaccurate recounting of Dominican history under Haitian military rule is still used today to whip up anti-Haitian hysteria. In truth, the Haitian occupation brought freedom to Dominican slaves and broke up the monopolization of land and wealth by colonizing Spain and the Catholic Church. Any mention of the Haitian occupation today in the Dominican Republic begins with a wild tale of vicious Haitian soldiers throwing children into the air and chopping them up with their machetes as they fell. We must struggle against this distorted historical memory which has been imposed on us and begin to rescue the Dominican and Haitian people's history of solidarity.

Why would an intellectual like Balaguer attack Haiti? Political opportunism. The Haitian people have long served as the easiest whipping boy. in the DR, easy to blame for social crisis. They are blamed for many things, from AIDS to unemployment. If it were not for these ideological escape valves, the manipulators of truth would have to invent another enemy or confront the structural dynamics of gross class and national inequalities in the Caribbean region.

Originally published in the newspaper Haïti Progres in Port-au-Prince Haiti in the summer of 2005.
http://www.haitiaction.net/News/HP/5_27_5.html

PASSAGE TO HAITI

This account, written last summer, reveals that the present crackdown in the Dominican Republic is but another chapter in the constant persecution of Haitians in that country.

Monday, August 16, 2004, was a day like any other for the more than 1,500,000 Haitians who call the Dominican Republic home. The majority were up by 6 a.m. with the sun and off to work in the tobacco, rice and sugarcane fields. The going wage for the Haitian laborers is 150 pesos, the equivalent of US$3.70 for 10 hours of heavy labor.

Nené and Juné didn't go to work that day. They had picked that day to travel back to Trou du Nord and Cap Haitien, their hometowns across the border in Haiti. They had been saving up their wages for several months and were anxious to return home and see their families. I sat in the back of the bus with them and 30 other Haitians. About fifteen Dominicans occupied the rest of the seats in the front listening to the bachata of Fran Reyes and paying little attention to the Kreyòl being spoken in the back. The driver roared over the dry countryside road known as La Linea, slowing only to avoid large tire-ruining holes.

The trip from Santiago, the Dominican Republic's second largest city, to Cap, Haiti's second capital, takes approximately seven hours by bus. I nestled down in my seat introducing myself to several new friends and taking vocabulary notes on various anecdotes and jokes in Kreyòl. There was no sign of trouble until about two hours into the trip when it was time to pay. The driver's partner, the *cobrador*, went around collecting the fare. I asked him several times the price of the trip but he refused to give an exact answer.

He collected 100 pesos from most of the passengers. The Haitians grew anxious as they waited for their change because they suspected they would be cheated. They protested. The driver stopped the bus and threatened to throw off any Haitians who wasn't quiet. Tension grew. The *cobrador* slapped Nené across the face a few times in a half-playful, half-mocking way and told him to sit down. It reminded me of the way masters probably slapped their house slaves not too long ago. I called the *cobrador* over and stayed calm. I put him in a light headlock and whispered to him that the jokes were over. If he wanted to slap somebody, I was right there, I said, but kindly keep his hands off everybody else.

I demanded that he declare the exact price to the Haitian border in order to sort out all of the confusion. I smiled and he began to give the Haitians their change. He moved toward the front of the bus. I thought we had broken bread but had gravely miscalculated the man's bitterness. He stood in the door of the bus and yelled back at me a few threats. I erupted and told him in several languages that a crook was a crook. At the next military checkpoint somewhere between Montecristi and Dajabon, he got off the bus and called the Colonel in charge of the military headquarters. Soon, a police chief and three soldiers were pleading with me to get off the bus, saying I had created a riotous situation. I refused. They were not sure what to do about me. Had I been Haitian, I would surely have had a few bullets pumped into me. But a North American tourist? A Westerner from a country of privilege? A white man? All the Haitians whispered to me: "Don't get off." I didn't intend to.

Then the chief and his three henchmen charged onto the bus, pushing through women and children. They tried to put cuffs on me but I wrestled. Machine guns were drawn, and I found the captain's .22 caliber piston to my head. The wrestling was over. They dragged a random Haitian man off the bus with me for good measure. I never caught his name nor saw him again. A few Dominican women who understood all too well the routine protested to the army that I wasn't in violation of any law. I appreciated their speaking up. But they were wrong. I had violated a deathly silence that resides across the Dominican Republic concerning Haitians and human rights.

As they dragged me away, I struggled to make one last point. Though the military and president Hipólito Mejía are to blame for the corruption and violence marking the roads to and from Haiti, every Dominican citizen and every citizen of the world who stays quiet in the face of this Apartheid also carries the responsibility. Duarte, Sanchez, Mella, Caamaño, and every other Dominican patriot would be ashamed. Haitians are not responsible for the miserable economic downturn the D.R. has taken in the past four years and for the past four centuries for that matter. They are simply the easiest scapegoat. A spent a few lonely hours in jail and bribed my way out. I imagine the Haitian who was detained did not sure the same luck that I did.

What transpired in the course of this journey was not unique. It was a microcosm of the everyday humiliation Haitians are subjected to in the neighboring country. The only difference was that I was there to witness what I hadn't seen in three years since I worked as an ethnographer and teacher in the Caribbean. I'm excited for everyone out there, we have recently graduated lawyers, journalists, and other professionals among us. May we continue to put our heads together to mobilize against the humiliations of imperialism everywhere.

Politricks Time Again

Resistanz

Lestè is struggling even by Haitian standards. Located a few hours north of Port-au-Prince, Lestè is an area that has been periodically ravaged by droughts, hurricanes and flash floods. There are stories of families who have ate dirt cookies to get through the famine. The geophagists warn of the damage that this can do to young tummies without asking why families are forced to resort to these survival tactics in the first place. Never is there any mention on *CNN* or in *USA Today* of the five-century long colonial earthquake that has shook and ravaged Haiti long before the natural disaster that occurred in January of 2012.

I first came to Lestè in the year 2000. I had met a Haitian friend Widson Etienne who was studying at a monastery in Santo Domingo where I was a teacher, journalist and organizer. We worked together in defense of Haitian's human and constitutional rights in the Dominican Republic. He invited me to travel with him and meet his family in Haiti. We developed some curriculum together that exposed Columbus and the rest of the colonial bandits for the rapists and tourists that they were. He had invited me to dialogue with some peasant organizations who were struggling against the privatization of their land. I learned a great deal from Widson's family and community.

Though I had fond memories of my visit, I was not able to return to Widson's village for many years. This past summer I found myself back in Haiti doing work against the UN occupation. It dawned on me that I was only a few hours north of Lestè. I did not call or give any advance notice to Widson's family of my arrival. I thought "Well what the heck? What is 14 years in the grand scheme of things?" In a city of only 40,000 someone is bound to know someone. Otherwise I can just make some new friends, right?

Lestè

Reunited

A pickup truck -functioning as a bus- transported us across a bridge marking the dividing point between Gonaive and Lestè. The bus ride was fun reminding me of the fascination many Haitians have with foreigners. There are a number of reasons for this. Haitians have been taught they are inferior. Many people see migration to the US -or really to anywhere outside of Haiti- as the only way to save themselves and their family. An average American's purchasing power is 100 to 300 times that of the average Haitian. Any interaction with a foreigner then is a step in the direction of hope.

Many Haitians have only seen foreigners in the world cup in a movie so they would compare me to television personalities. Some kids said I looked like Zinedine Zidane -the Algerian soccer player- while others argued that I was a clone of Jean Claude Van Damme the actor. Haiti is good for one's self-esteem in that way, you always get compared to somebody famous.

The skies were overcast and I inquire if rain is upon us. "No. It never rains here" is the reply. I forgot where to get off to find my old friends. I waited until there was a big gathering of people and I dismounted the vehicle. A traveling companion inquires if I know where I am going? I respond with a feigned confidence "Yeah I'll figure it out." I take 3 steps and ask a young man with headphones and a hoody if he knows Widson Etienne. His face lights up. "That is my uncle. Is that you Dan-yel? It is me Samson." Jackpot! I knew I could track the old crew down but I never thought it would be that easy. It was almost a letdown. Part of the adventure is being lost in time, in another galaxy. Three steps and three seconds? I thought I would have to dig a bit more. Samson skipped his return to Gonaives to study and led me back to his family's home.

As we walked through the market, the cutest 2 1/2 year old tike appeared by my side and took my hand. You would swear he was my nephew the way he latched on to me. "Where is his mother?" I asked Samson. Why is he clenching my hand and walking with me? We were now 10 minutes walking from where I found him. Samson told me his name was Ti-Ralph, laughing and assuring me our new-found companion would eventually find his way back home. We picked up an assortment of Haitian fruits, including a watermelon with the seeds in tact which you can rarely find in the US now-a-days.

Ti-Ralph

We reached Widson's home. I had not seen them in over 10 years but they instantly recognized me. They welcomed me back into their home. I sat down and we began to reminisce. They asked me all about Widson and his beautiful wife and children in Hartford, Connecticut. They took me in like family. Neighbors and their children gravitated over to the house to see what the commotion was. A friend from far away was big news in Lestè.

It was time for a shower. There are different notions of privacy in the countryside. Granmè or Nana Yvonne gave me a bucket of water and instructed me to bathe in a little makeshift chamber right behind where the children were playing and the adults were preparing dinner. I was just out of the view of three generations of a family and I was expected to shower. Tonton Makenley struck up a conversation with me about Haitian women as I bathed. "Do you like them? How are they in bed? Sweet aren't they?" I could only laugh as I carried on with my business. I guess you become accustomed to having less privacy. Going to the bathroom was similar. People just didn't look. But sometimes children wandered around out of nowhere and began to stare at me in compromising moments.

No shower ever felt as cleansing as a bucket shower after taking on the dust and devastating sun of Okap Aysyen. A majestic peace that came over me as I sat down to share some dinner with my long-lost family and enjoy the evening serenity.

A Quiet Night Interrupted

Barely thirty minutes had elapsed when they passed me a cell phone. Widson's brother and other nephew motioned for me to bring it to my ear. I heard a familiar voice in Kreyol half yelling and half laughing at me on the other end: "You white bastard who doesn't bathe you! Why didn't you tell me you were going to Haiti you old vagabond! You have ruined my life." It was Widson calling from Hartford, Connecticut. He has discovered that I was back in his hometown. So much for my quiet entrance and departure. My cover was blown.

Election Time

Did I mention that Widson was running for national senator in representation of Lestè? No. I chose to forget that. The elections were supposed to have happened two years ago but since the illegal ouster of the democratically elected president Jean Bertrand Aristide and his kidnapping by US marines, elections have been suspended. As the October date approached the 28 different candidates for one position were shoring up all of the support they could get. I feared he wanted to enroll an American professor in his campaign.

The pleasantries were over. He began to feed me instructions: "Danyel you are a white man. People listen to white men in my town. You must go out and campaign for me. Do you drive stick? If not no problem. I am sending for a car for you now. Do you want your own driver?" I can't keep up with the bombardment of questions. "What are you wearing? When do you depart for Port-au-Prince? Can you campaign for me there? I will have my cousin pick you up. Do you need a cell phone? Do you need money? Women? How many women do you want?"

A quiet night visiting old friends and cracking jokes was suddenly transformed into a campaign opportunity. I listened to my orders intently. He sent me out with my campaign team. What had I got myself into? Wait I never consented to any of this. And what about our watermelon? Forever the adventurer, I think to myself "Ah why not? Let me see how long I can ride this out before I compromise my principles. Roll with the punches, right?"

We were off. A Suzuki jeep swept us up and we sped away. I turned, waved goodbye and blew a kiss to everyone but no one could see me through the tinted windows. The driver cranked the AC all the way up, the perfect contrast to the sleepless humidity on the other side of the tinted windows. The kompa blared out. From rags to riches in a matter of seconds. Momentarily I felt how Rick Ross must feel. I liked the "boss" lifestyle. One phone call shifted my destiny. Excitement was in the air. I'm somebody. I'm taken care of. We doesn't want to be a made-man? We passed by some homes to pick up some other "members" of the "team." Our chauffeur George, Widson's cousin, slowed all the way down and called the "volunteers" over. He introduced me as a campaign boss from New York who had been sent over to supervise their activity. I reached over the chauffer's body to extend a hand to our volunteer team. They assured me they were working their hardest as one hid a bottle of *kleren* or moonshine behind his back.

We continued making the rounds. In many areas of Haiti, once the sun goes down there is no electricity. George's headlights along with candles lit up local homes where some *akasan* and *griyo* was being sold. *Akasan* is a sweet corn-based hot beverage. *Griyo* are slices of fried pork served with fried plantain. Throngs of young men -hanging out on a bridge in the pitch darkness- gathered around us. People saluted one another through the darkness and I wondered how they recognized each other. I could not see 5 feet in front of me. I shook so many hands I thought I was running for office. I was presented as some type of celebrity. Suddenly I was again whisked away and then deposited in front of a local disco and introduced to a group of 15 men hanging out on the sidewalk. The disco was completely empty. No one had the money to afford the cover and cold beverages served inside. All eyes were on me and I am introduced as Widsons' right-hand man.

A Tribune of the People

I introduced myself and explained my mission in Haiti; to learn to listen to write to grow to share. I quickly launched into my usual berating of foreigners who exploit Haiti. I knew that I was supposed to sing praises to our candidate and promise whole-sale change to one of the most exploited corners of the western hemisphere. My heart refused to follow orders. My own political training kicked in. "Politicians play games of false promises and politricks." "Mwen pa konfye avek politik yo. Mwen konfye ann pep-la. Se selma pep-la ki ka sove pep-la. Ki sa ki Dessalines toujou ap di. Nou beswen yon lot dechoukaj." ("I don't trust politicians. I trust the people. Only the people can save the people. What did Dessalines teach us? Only the united masses can effect deep-rooted change. Radical! That means to lift things up from the roots. That is the only change I believe in.") George tugged at my arm. "Ok Dan-yel time to get going. Say bye to everyone." "But George I am just getting started" I retorted.

The crowd is fired up and we are all having fun. I redefined what it means to be a politician. I paraphrased Amilcar Cabral and his explanation of what it means to be a revolutionary. "We always should say what is. Honesty is first and foremost. We cannot make promises but rather chart out what it will take for a united people to make gains through struggle. A real leader of the people does not aspire for anything for himself. He aspires for everything for everyone. "A tribune of the people," a re-imagined, re-defined "politician" responds to everyone's pain making connections between the struggles of battered women, landless peasants, irate students, slum dwellers and every other oppressed group.[1]

My instinct was to lump insult Haitian politicians who sold out into my invective. But I learned a valuable lesson on prior occasions. It is ok to insult foreign devils but leave their local sycophants and puppets alone. You never know whose territory you are in. You never know who pays whose salary and who wants revenge against who. On another occasion in Site Sole - Port-au-Prince's sprawling slums that constitute the largest ghetto in the world- the political bosses of the local gangs pressed guns to my head for committing this misstep. That is a story for another time but the lesson was clear: focus your harangues on the foreign bloodsuckers.

By this time George has grabbed my arm trying to lead me away. The crowd cheered and the youth threw up some fists. The Rastas in the crowd wanted to hear more of the white man's denunciation of Babylon.

In the last exchange I knew that I had not even mentioned our dear candidate's name. Nor would I. They wanted to manipulate and hustle me but I had thrown a wrench in their political machine. I guess just the mere presence of the white man somehow connected to Widson was still worth some political capital because we were off to our next campaign stop. But not before George passed me the cellphone and I was again admonished by my would-be sponsor.

[1] Term coined by Vladimir Lenin in What is to Be Done?

Originally published in Liberation News on April 20th 2015.
https://www.liberationnews.org/aids-the-racist-blame-game-haitian-resistance-2/

AIDS, the Racist Blame Game and Haitian Resistance

Haiti's calendar is emblazoned with glorious dates of popular victory over slavery, racism and foreign occupation. Jan. 1 of this year was the 211th anniversary of the Haitian people's triumph over the French empire and their colonial allies who attempted to reestablish slavery in Haiti. July of this year will mark the 100th anniversary of the U.S. occupation of Haiti and the steadfast resistance of the Haitian masses led by the Caco leader Charlmagne Peralte. April 20 marked the 25th anniversary of a massive movement that erupted in the Haitian American community in 1990 after the Center for Disease Control published a study blaming Haitians, homosexuals, hemophiliacs and heroin users for the transmission of AIDS in the United States.

The anti-imperialist, national-unity newspaper Haiti Liberté hosted an evening of commemoration in Brooklyn to remember the mass movement that came into the streets 25 years ago to demand that Haitians be removed from this list. A passionate panel of speakers remembered the intensity of the April days and the campaign to unite everyone against the prevailing racism at the time which equated Haitians with AIDS. According to the research of medical anthropologist Dr. Paul Farmer and others, AIDS was introduced from the U.S. into Haiti, but this was never convenient for the mainstream news long-accustomed to unscientific claims which scapegoated African and African-descended peoples for the spread of disease. [1]

Half a million Haitians and their supporters came into the streets on April 20, 1990, marching through their Flatbush neighborhoods in Brooklyn to City Hall making the Brooklyn Bridge shake as it had never shook before. Due to the massive mobilization, the CDC was forced to retract their racist claim. Racism was turned back by the power and unity of the people.

Community leader and journalist Berthony Dupont reminded the crowd: "We are at war. Haiti is at war. They have never stopped waging war against us. They cannot forgive us for overthrowing their rule and demanding our freedom." He drew a parallel to the introduction of cholera into Haiti by UN troops who today illegally occupy Haiti. The outbreak of cholera has thus far left over 4,000 Haitians dead and the UN has yet to recognize its role in polluting the Haitian water supply and spreading this disease.

Haitian women leaders who were in high school at the time remembered the intense anti-Haitian sentiment that they confronted on a daily basis. One Haitian nurse exclaimed: "They made us ashamed to be Haitian. They said HBO stood for Haitian Body Odor. Haiti was only mentioned in association with coups, violence, hunger and disease. We had to learn to love ourselves. We had to stand up. This mobilization was a key part of our learning to love ourselves and be proud of our identity when we were attacked from all angles." Waving her fist defiantly, she concluded, "Again we had to teach our detractors: You don't mess with Haitians!"

April 20 and all of Haiti's history reiterates the timeless adage that has rung true from Belfast to Port-au-Prince to Ho Chi Minh City: "Repression breeds resistance. Resistance brings freedom." The Party for Socialism and Liberation salutes the Haitian people for all that they have sacrificed and won for oppressed people everywhere and pledges to stand strong against our common enemy here in the belly of the beast!

---

[1] Farmer, Paul. <u>Aids and Accusations: The Geography of Blame</u>. 2006

Originally published in Haiti Liberté March 15ᵗʰ, 2015

http://www.haiti-liberte.com/archives/volume8-36/Fifteen%20Years%20Ago.asp

Fifteen Years Ago, the Killing and Funeral of Haitian-American Patrick Dorismond, Shot by Undercover NYPD Cops

The Day Flatbush Exploded

Mar. 16, 2000 was a day like any other for Patrick Dorismond. He worked his shift as a security guard at the 34th Street Partnership in Manhattan and went to have a beer with a coworker after work at the Wakamba Cocktail Lounge. He was in a good mood because the next day was payday.

As Patrick left the bar after midnight, some middle-aged men approached him trying to score some marijuana. Patrick politely told them he didn't do drugs and asked them to keep it moving. They insisted that surely he knew where they could score. The situation escalated until Patrick's voice rose, warning the troublemakers to get lost.

The men were undercover NYPD officers instructed to "bring in the dope-peddling good-for-nothings." Patrick, a 26-year-old Haitian-American whose parents had immigrated to Brooklyn, fit the cops' profile of a "good-for-nothing," and they planned to fulfill their quota. Without identifying themselves, the cops attacked the security guard. When Patrick defended himself , two other back-up officers – called "ghosts" – intervened, shooting him in the chest, killing him instantly.

Patrick Dorismond, a 26-year-old Haitian-American, was shot dead by undercover NYPD cops on Mar. 17, 2000 after he yelled at them for badgering him about where to buy illegal drugs

That night, Patrick did not go home to his fiancée Karen and their one-year-old daughter Destiny. To the naïve, the shooting was a terrible isolated tragedy. But the Black community knew this was police "business as usual," endured by Black people for decades. Mayor Rudolph Giuliani attacked the victim, claiming Dorismond was at fault and "no altar boy," never once expressing regret for the loss of an innocent life. Interestingly enough, Patrick had attended the same Brooklyn Catholic school – Immaculate Heart of Mary – as the mayor, an irony Giuliani chose to ignore. As the funeral approached, tension was high between a community outraged by police abuse and a police department drunk with arrogance and racism.

Would We Patrol Your Funerals?
Thousands converged in Brooklyn two weekends after Patrick's murder to stand with his family and express their repudiation of the latest police slaying. The somber funeral procession on Sat., Mar. 25, 2000 grew in size and anger as it slowly rolled up Flatbush Avenue, a central artery of the Haitian community. By the time the march reached Holy Cross Church where the funeral was held, an ocean of humanity filled Church Avenue. The police were clearly alarmed at the size of the crowd. The air was heavy with grief and anger. Young and old alike looked into the police officers' faces as if to say: "Why are you even here? This is not your family's affair. Go back to where you came from, and let us grieve. Would we patrol your funerals?"

It was clear that Flatbush was on the brink of combustion. The spark that ignited the crowd came in the form of yet another police miscalculation. Dorismond's body was taken out of the church's back door and loaded into a hearse, which started toward the cemetery for burial. The crowd of thousands wanted to quietly and respectfully follow the casket, but the police stopped them. A melee ensued as the furious crowd demanded to accompany Patrick to his final resting place. One, two, or three confrontations soon mushroomed into hundreds. Rocks and bottles flew. The police lost control of the situation, and found themselves surrounded by and drowning in a sea of fury. White-shirted police captains barked into their walkie talkies, chaos enveloping them.

The terrain had shifted under the feet of the invaders. The indigenous army grew emboldened. The ranks of the enraged swelled with fresh recruits, who streamed in from surrounding streets. Police reinforcements also arrived, chasing the mourners turned demonstrators, but they were in hostile territory. Every doorway was an entrance to a hallway that became an escape tunnel. When the cops tried to close in on prey, a door magically opened, snatching the children from their would-be wardens.

Thousands marched alongside the funeral cortege of Patrick Dorismond on Mar. 25, 2000. Shortly later, the mourners were in pitched battles with the police

Demonstrators clashed with police after they were prevented from accompanying Patrick Dorismond's casket to the cemetery

Two armies engaged each other on a battlefield called Church Avenue. One was motivated to collect their paychecks and appease their superiors. The other sought to undo and transform years of humiliation into a united fightback. A 15-year-old boy – born in Port-au-Prince but reared in Brooklyn – would later claim that Haitians were born with rocks in their back pockets precisely for these moments of self-defense.

Next, the police cavalry was deployed. In unison, the multitude burst into a chant: "Get those animals off those horses!" A young man-child ran straight at the approaching enemy lines, did an about face, dropped his drawers, and mooned the cops to the applause and cheers of the mighty crowd. The move struck a chord with the generation of youth warriors. As if rehearsed, the cadre of teenagers saluted their oncoming foes with this perfectly-timed gesture of contempt, signaling a fresh rain of glass, steel, and stone on the police. The horses were turned back. Some mounted cops fell, reduced to a state of atomized desperation.

This was the closest some would ever get to emancipation. Powerlessness dislodged power. Regardless of the aftermath, for that brief moment, oppressed people controlled the situation, their environment, their humanity. Every demonstrator's smile posed the question: How does it feel, boys, to try to wade into the mighty current of the people's wrath? Those accustomed to swaggering with full confidence now retreated in full sprints, thinking of their own families and loved ones. Were there human feelings beneath those uniforms and badges?

An NBC news crew wanted to be the first major television network to break the story. The camera crew piled out of the news truck intent upon recording the situation and interviewing the balaclava-clad rebels. They immediately came under fire from a group of young generals who bombarded the news truck with bottles and rocks. Sprinting in high-heals and Dockers, the once-confident news-crew raced back to their van and then sped off with shattered windows and windshield. The masses burst into laughter waving "Bon voyage," as if to say surely you can misreport from a safe distance, up in your helicopters and your air-conditioned newsrooms. It is not safe for you down here in the street where history unfolds.

Time and again, youths threw bricks and bottles from alleys and rooftops. Time and again, phalanxes of police turned and ran. The underdog was winning.

How many years of accumulated rage detonated that day? The ancestors of the Haitians outside Holy Cross Church that day had risen up against slavery and colonialism and defeated Napoleon's legions, the mightiest army in that time. Now their Haitian descendants, the daughters and sons of Dessalines, Capois La Mort, and Toussaint L'Ouverture, showed us how to stand up to those who think they are invincible. They showed all of Brooklyn and the oppressed around the world that we all have a Haiti within, searching for redemption.

Resistance to Injustice is Justified

The masses bid farewell to Patrick Dorismond with valiant resistance, assuring that he had not died in vain and promising Guilianni to rache manyòk li – uproot him from office. Dorismond's murder – coming on the heals of the August 1997 torture of Abner Louima and the February 1999 murder of Amadou Diallo – and the police force's heavy-hand at his funeral were two drops which made the cup of people's anger overflow. The police had a taste of the fear of violence their victims live with day in and day out.

"Our best organizers in the South," the reverend Dr. Martin Luther King Jr. once said, "are the police themselves." Giuliani's NYPD proved this once again in March 2000.

Some might tell us not to glorify violent resistance and to limit ourselves to hand-wringing when faced with police abuse and aggression, so often lethal. But nothing has ever stopped oppressors in their tracks like organized self-defense, which is sometimes spontaneous. We should not rule out non-violence and civil disobedience. All are viable and valid tactics in the pursuit of freedom.

In the words of Guyanese freedom-fighter Walter Rodney: "the revolution will be as peaceful as possible and as violent as necessary." Only the victimized and oppressed can determine which weapon is correct at each confrontation with their brutalizers. Those on the sidelines – comfortable with sermonizing – should stay right there as the people take center stage in standing up against injustice, just as they did 15 years ago.

About the Author

Danny Shaw teaches Latin American and Caribbean Studies and Race, Ethnicity, Class and Gender at the City University of New York. He holds a Masters in International Affairs from the School of International and Public Affairs at Columbia University. He was born and raised by a single mother in Brockton, Massachusetts and has lived in the Bronx for the past 18 years. He is fluent in Spanish, Haitian Kreyol, Portuguese, Cape Verdean Kreolu and has a fair command of French. He has worked and organized in forty different countries, opening his spirit to countless testimonies about the inhumanity of the international economic system. He is a Golden Gloves boxer, fighting twice in Madison Square Garden for the NYC heavyweight championship. He teaches boxing, yoga and nutrition. He works in the national leadership of the ANSWER Coalition (Act Now to Stop War and End Racism) to keep young people out of the military and prison industrial complex. He is a mentor to many guiding them through the nutritional, ideological, social and emotional landmines that surround us. He is the father of two young Life Warriors, Ernesto Rafael and Caũa Amaru. He is the author of five books: 365 Days of Resistance, Shedding that which is Not Us: A Working-Class Guide to Life Foods Training and Healing, The Saints of Santo Domingo: Dominican Resistance in the Age of Neocolonialism, My Son Blazes within Me: Reflections on a Poor "white" Family's Survival, and Diving over Infinite Horizons: Journal Entries of an Internationalist. He has also authored blogs and articles on Latin American history, boxing and nutrition, among other topics. He can be contacted at DRS33@Columbia.edu.

60897584R00135

Made in the USA
Charleston, SC
08 September 2016